Samuel Pepys's
SPANISH PLAYS

Samuel Pepys's
SPANISH PLAYS

EDWARD M. WILSON
&
DON W. CRUICKSHANK

LONDON
THE BIBLIOGRAPHICAL SOCIETY
1980

Oxford University Press, Walton Street, Oxford OX2 6DP
London Glasgow New York Toronto
Delhi Bombay Calcutta Madras Karachi
Kuala Lumpur Singapore Hong Kong Tokyo
Nairobi Dar es Salaam Cape Town
Melbourne Wellington
and associate companies in
Beirut Berlin Ibadan Mexico City
Published in the United States by
Oxford University Press, New York

BIBLIOGRAPHICAL SOCIETY PUBLICATION
FOR THE YEARS 1977 AND 1978
PUBLISHED 1980

British Library Cataloguing in Publication Data
Wilson, Edward Meryon
Samuel Pepys's Spanish plays. – (Bibliographical Society. Publications).
1. Pepys, Samuel – Library
2. Spanish drama – Classical period, 1500–1700 – History and criticism
I. Title II. Cruickshank, Don William
III. Series
862'.3'09 Z997.P42/

ISBN 0-19-721793-1

Printed in Great Britain
by The Scolar Press Ilkley West Yorkshire

CONTENTS

The Council of the Bibliographical Society is most grateful to Lionel Robinson, Esq, CBE, MC, and to Philip Robinson, Esq, for their generous gifts towards the cost of publication of this monograph.

PREFACE

THE history of this monograph begins in 1953, when Edward Wilson moved from the chair of Spanish at King's College, London, to that of the University of Cambridge. In Cambridge he found time to undertake a lengthy examination of Pepys 1545, a volume of *pliegos sueltos* (chap-books) collected by Samuel Pepys in Spain. He had known of the volume before; Sir Stephen Gaselee drew particular attention to it on p. 15 of *The Spanish books in the library of Samuel Pepys*, published as a supplement by the Bibliographical Society in 1921. The main fruits of that examination appeared in the *Transactions of the Cambridge Bibliographical Society* between 1955 and 1957. The history of the texts was studied, authors were identified, and imprintless *pliegos* assigned dates and printers on the basis of recurring woodblocks. Wilson then turned to Pepys 1553, a volume of Spanish plays, to which Gaselee had also drawn attention. None of these plays had an imprint, and most had no woodblocks; he found that copies held by other libraries had somewhat improbable guess-dates assigned to them by cataloguers – improbable, given that Pepys had acquired the contents of the volume in 1684. The investigation would obviously be a lengthy one and, having other projects on hand, he postponed it.

When I came to Dublin in 1970, after five years in Cambridge, my new head of department, Professor P. Gallagher, told me of a collection of old editions of Calderón plays in one of the city's libraries. They contained one woodblock associated with a printer I had already worked on. This was scarcely conclusive, but a full typographical examination showed that he had indeed printed eight of the plays. Edward Wilson helped and advised me throughout the work, and we eventually published it together in the 1974 issue of *Long Room*. This minor success reminded him of the unsolved problem of Pepys 1553, and when I saw him in England in March 1974, he turned over to me his file on the plays' printers. Meanwhile, he restarted his own work on the history of the plays and their authors. By the summer of 1976, he had produced what is now Chapter V, while I had produced Chapter III. Several friends read what we had written, while we considered what to do with it, since it was already much too long for an article. One friend, Dr Derek Brewer (now Master of Emmanuel College), asked if he might publish it as a monograph. We readily agreed and by January 1977 produced a second draft in readiness for a printers' estimate. When the estimate came, it was twice what we had hoped, and the project hung fire again. In April 1977 Mr A. R. A. Hobson read our second draft and suggested that the Bibliographical Society might publish it, and also suggested ways in which we might broaden the work's scope. That summer Edward Wilson wrote Chapter IV and I wrote Chapter II. As we had done throughout, we sent each other what we had written for suggestions and comments. The last few pages of Chapter IV reached me early in October; a few days later a message sent through a friend asked me not to send on any comments for the time being, as he did not feel well enough to deal with them. He died on November 21.

I have made one or two additions to Chapter IV, but apart from these the book is a real piece of collaboration, in that every word written by one of us was read and approved by the other. A great many friends and colleagues, whose help and encouragement were invaluable, have also read it in whole or in part: their names are among those recorded at the end of Chapter V.

I do not know whom Edward would have chosen to dedicate the book to; but I should like to dedicate my share of it to his memory.

DWC

CHAPTER ONE

The Volume Pepys 1553

THE volume Pepys 1553 consists of twenty-six separate Spanish plays and two pamphlets. The plays are of the kind Spaniards call *sueltas*; they consist of three or four or more gatherings, with head-titles. The text is mostly in double columns. None has either date or imprint. The purpose of this monograph is to describe the plays in some detail in order that scholars who work in other libraries may identify any of these that they may come across, to discover (as far as possible) dates and printers and to throw some light on questions of authorship and identification. Some of these texts may be unique. Any of them may conceivably have important textual variants.

Pepys was in Cadiz and Seville between December 1683 and February 1684. In 1699–1701 his nephew, John Jackson, travelled abroad and was in Cadiz in October 1700. He also visited Madrid and Seville before he arrived back in England in July 1701. Jackson bought books for his uncle, but Gaselee says: 'I have no definite evidence that he bought anything there for the library – no new books, certainly, for none have so late a date as this.'[1] Among Pepys's Tangier papers in the Bodleian is an inventory of the contents of the 'Box Great' that he brought back with him to England in 1684; in it there are the items 'Pamphl^ts Plays Sermons &c.' and 'Bundle of Ballads'.[2] As has

[1] [Sir] Stephen Gaselee, *The Spanish books in the library of Samuel Pepys*, Oxford, 1921, p. 13.

[2] E. M. Wilson, 'Samuel Pepys's Spanish chap-books', *Transactions of the Cambridge Bibliographical Society*, II, ii (1955), 127–54; iii (1956), 229–68; iv (1957), 305–22. The plate mentioned here is opposite p. 130 in the 1955 number.

been shown elsewhere, the 'ballads' were almost certainly those now in volume 1545; the forty-two dated ones were printed between 1670 and 1683.[3] The plays and pamphlets must therefore have been those now in volume 1553. One of the pamphlets was printed in Seville in 1682. None of the plays is likely to have been printed after 1684.

Few items in volume 1553 have page numbers. The volume has been paged in pencil from 1 to 944, probably by the same hand who compiled the table of contents in the guard-leaves.[4] It is headed: 'Catalogo de las Comedias contenidas en el Libro siguiente'. The titles, authors and pages follow below it.

Our descriptions in Chapter V are given in the order in which they occur in the volume. We begin with the head-title and incipit of the play. Generally the words 'Jornada primera' seem to go with the head-title rather than with the incipit. But where these words appear as the heading only of the left-hand column of the text we have shifted them to the incipit. We then give notes of the make-up of each item, followed by the running headlines and the catchwords that occur at the end of each gathering. Then we quote the last two lines of the play itself and note the final ornament where there is one. Finally we give a conjectural date and printer's name.

We disregard the written-in pagination of the volume. The items in the book are listed here in the order given and with the name of the supposed author:

1	Don Francisco Balcarcel y Lugo	*El premio en la tirania*
2	Don Agustin Moreto	*San Franco de Sena*
3		*Los lagos de San Vicente*[5]
4	Don Cristoval de Monroy y Silva	*La sirena del Iordan San Iuan Baptista*

[3] Wilson, 'Samuel Pepys's Spanish chap-books', ii, 128.

[4] Mr D. Pepys-Whiteley told us that the hand is almost certainly that of Thomas Henderson.

[5] No author's name occurs in the head-title; in the running headlines he is named: M. Tirso de Molina.

5	Lope de Vega Carpio	*La creacion del mundo y primera culpa del hombre*
6	Don Pedro Calderon	*El esclavo de Maria*
7	Don Antonio de Mendoza	*El premio de la virtud, y sucessos prodigiosos de don Pedro Guerrero*
8	Francisco Ximenez Sedeño	*La aurora del Sol divino*
9	Don Pedro Calderon	*La exaltacion de la Cruz*
10	Don Pedro Calderon	*Las cadenas del demonio*
11	El alferez Jacinto Cordero	*El juramento ante Dios, y lealtad contra el amor*
12	Don Francisco de Roxas	*La segunda Magdalena, y sirena de Napoles*
13	D. Francisco de la Torre	*La azuzena de Etiopia*
14	Alvaro Cubillo	*El mejor rey del mundo, y templo de Salomon*
15	El maestro Tirso de Molina	*El condenado por desconfiado*
16	Don Sebastian de Olivares	*Guardar palabra a los santos*
17	Don Christoval de Monroy y Silva	*El gigante cananeo*
18	Lope de Vega Carpio	*El animal profeta*
19	El Doctor Juan Perez de Montalvan	*El divino portugues San Antonio de Padua*
20	Lope de Vega Carpio	*El milagro por los zelos*
21	Don Pedro Calderon	*El angel de la guarda*
22	Don Pedro Calderon	*El mejor padre de pobres*
23	Lope de Vega Carpio	*La obediencia laureada*
24	Don Francisco de Roxas	*No ay dicha, ni desdicha hasta la muerte*
25	Don Francisco de Roxas	*Los trabajos de Tobias. La nueva*
26	El Doctor Juan Perez de Montalvan	*Santa Maria Egipciaca, y gitana de Menfis*
27	El doct. D. Francisco de Prada	*Vejamen . . .*
28	D. Christoval Francisco de Luque	*Vejamen . . .*

No. 28 is the only work with an imprint contained in this volume. The last *Vejamen* was printed by Juan Francisco de Blas for Pedro de Santiago, bookseller, presumably in 1682, for it records the proceedings which took place on 29 April of that year. The other *Vejamen* (no. 27) has no imprint, but the record is of 27 December 1675.

CHAPTER TWO

Printing and the Book Trade in Seville up to 1700

SEVILLE is unusual among Spanish cities in that printing was introduced there by Spaniards, not by foreigners. As early as 1477 (and possibly before) a press was set up by Antonio Martínez, Bartolomé Segura and Alfonso del Puerto. The partnership did not survive long, however, and within ten years printing at Seville had entirely ceased. In 1490–1 the Catholic Monarchs invited two foreign firms to set up shop in the city. The first firm consisted of four Germans, who usually styled themselves the 'Cuatro compañeros alemanes', the second of a German (Meinardo Ungut) and of a Pole (Stanislao Polono). Ungut and Polono first established themselves in the Calle de Génova, in the parish of Santa María. Their work-force may have included a German named Jacob Cromberger, who was to become the greatest and best-known of Seville's printers.[1]

Ungut died in 1499, and between that date and 1503 Cromberger married his widow and became the partner of Stanislao Polono. In 1504 Stanislao stopped printing, leaving Cromberger in sole possession of the firm. Cromberger was fortunate: the time and place were particularly propitious for expansion of the book trade. Even before 1492 Seville had been the most prosperous city in Castile, as well as its largest port. Once

[1] For a more detailed account of Seville printing up to 1520, see the *Catalogue of books printed in the XVth century now in the British Museum, Part X, Spain and Portugal*, London, 1971, pp. lii–lvi; and F. J. Norton, *Printing in Spain 1501–1520*, Cambridge, 1966, pp. 8–19.

America had been discovered, and Seville granted the trade monopoly, the city became the fastest-growing one in Castile, in terms both of commerce and of population. The best-known authority on this period of Spanish printing has said that 'the book trade flourished there as it did nowhere else in the Castilian area'.[2] At an early stage Cromberger became a publisher in the modern sense, and a bookseller; by 1511 he had acquired the monopoly for liturgical works in the diocese of Seville; the following year he was paid 4000 *maravedís* for reading primers destined for the New World. He also printed books for the Portuguese market, both in Seville and in Portugal itself, and it was during a trip to Lisbon in 1528 that he died. His descendants continued printing until the 1550s.[3]

Cromberger had his counterparts in other major Spanish cities, and was in contact with many of them. Surviving documents indicate that many of these men were prosperous, even wealthy, and that they carried out many of the processes in the book trade themselves; that is, they owned matrices, in which they cast their own type; they could afford to act as their own publishers; and they owned retail outlets, which often comprised binderies. Only in matrices and paper were they not self-sufficient.

In the course of the sixteenth century the Spanish printing industry expanded enormously. In the second half of the century the printers changed, as their neighbours in France and Italy had done earlier, from gothic to roman type. The native punch-cutting industry, such as it was, was unable to meet the demand caused by this change, and both matrices and type were imported from abroad, mainly from France, by then Europe's chief type-producer, and from the Spanish Netherlands. The better, more conscientious printers tried hard but not always successfully to buy or at least to borrow good matrices: the unsuccessful attempts made by Matthew Gast, a Fleming

[2] Norton, *Printing in Spain* . . ., p. 6.

[3] Norton, *Printing in Spain* . . ., pp. 10–14.

working in Salamanca, to acquire matrices for two Garamont romans, seem to be typical.[4] Printers with lower standards or less capital had to buy cast type, either from their more prosperous colleagues or from specialist typefounders.

Evidence of the manner in which Seville printers obtained type during this period is circumstantial rather than documentary. Documents indicate that the typefounder Antonio de Espinosa and his assistant Diego de Montoya were induced in 1550 by financial considerations to leave Seville for Mexico City. The value of their services can be judged from the fact that Espinosa was given a three-year contract at 150 gold ducats a year, Montoya forty-eight ducats a year. Board and lodging, and the passage to Mexico, were to be free.[5] Espinosa later printed in Mexico on his own account, from 1559 to 1575.

Less than half a century later Seville printers were sending to Madrid for type. In late 1596 or early 1597 the Seville printer Rodrigo de Cabrera (active *c.* 1595–9) himself went to Madrid to buy type from the founder Francisco de Robles in order to print Juan de Pineda's commentary on Job. Cabrera bought type to the value of 1856 *reales* (169 ducats), but the cost was met by one of the author's colleagues, not by Cabrera himself. The first volume of the book appeared in 1598 (Escudero 806, a large folio).[6]

[4] D. W. Cruickshank, 'Some aspects of Spanish book-production in the Golden Age', *The Library*, V, xxxi (1976), 5–6.

[5] J. Gestoso y Pérez, *Noticias inéditas de impresores sevillanos*, Seville, 1924, pp. 115–17; also I. B. Iguiniz, 'La imprenta en México durante la dominación española', *Gutenberg Festschrift*, Mainz, 1925, p. 123. Braudel quotes an estimated income of forty-four ducats *per family* per year in Castilian villages in the 1570s; he reckons up to twenty ducats per year as a 'subsistence' wage, and from twenty to forty as a 'small' wage (*The Mediterranean and the Mediterranean world in the age of Philip II*, London, 1972, 2 vols., i, 456–8).

[6] C. Pérez Pastor, *Bibliografía madrileña*, Madrid, 1891–1907, 3 vols., iii, 454; for a description of the book, see F. Escudero y Perosso, *Tipografía hispalense*, Madrid, 1894, item 806 (further references to Escudero give his name and the item number).

In 1603 the printer Clemente Hidalgo of Seville told the author Fray Luis de Rebolledo that he was ready to print the second part of his *Coronica de San Francisco* 'en letra de testo que agora la fundio nueva francisco de robles para el dho libro' (in great primer newly cast by Francisco de Robles [of Madrid] for the aforesaid book). We do not know how many copies Hidalgo was printing, but he reckoned the length of the book at 200 sheets (it has 177: see Escudero 876), and promised that he would print two sheets per day, using two presses.[7] In 1605 Gabriel Ramos Vejarano, who was then working in Córdoba but was later to move to Seville, also obtained cast type from Robles.[8] It seems likely that typefounding in Seville had declined, possibly to extinction, certainly to the point of being unable to meet local requirements.

Circumstantial evidence in support of this decline is more numerous, if less convincing. It takes the form of Flemish typefaces which were rare or less common in other parts of Spain, or which apparently reached Seville first. One of these is Guyot's *médiane italique*, which was not common even in the Low Countries. Vervliet records that it first appeared in 1553 and that it had reached Lisbon by 1557.[9] With no more than a cursory glance we have found it in books printed by Andrea Pescioni in Seville in 1582, one of them the *Algunas obras* of Fernando de Herrera, *el divino*. (The ports of Lisbon and Seville, it may be remembered, were the Peninsula's principal trading links with Antwerp.) To the best of our knowledge, this

[7] Gestoso y Pérez, *Noticias inéditas . . .*, pp. 143–5. Two presses imply four pressmen; and since one folio page of great primer contains 1600–1900 ens, two sheets (eight pages) contain 12,800–15,200 ens. This represents at least a whole day's setting for two average compositors. So Hidalgo's work-force presumably numbered at least six.

[8] J. M. Valdenebro y Cisneros, *La imprenta en Córdoba*, Madrid, 1900, p. xvii, n. 4.

[9] H. D. L. Vervliet, *Sixteenth-century printing types of the Low Countries*, Amsterdam, 1968, p. 301. All the evidence suggests that Guyot catered for the export market. His 1565 specimen is annotated in English.

italic was not used in Madrid until the 1680s. Guyot's *ascendonica italique* (double pica) is rare in Spain. It seems to occur first in books printed in Madrid by Lucas Antonio de Bedmar between 1670 and 1675; it is battered and worn even in 1670. Significantly, perhaps, Bedmar had moved to Madrid from Seville shortly before, apparently bringing type with him. Guyot's *médiane romaine* is even rarer than his *médiane italique*, but Hernando Díaz of Seville had it in 1575, and Pescioni in 1582. We have not seen it elsewhere in Spain. Guyot's *ascendonica romaine* seems to have been used almost everywhere except Madrid. Cut about 1544, it was in use in Lisbon by 1557, in Japan by 1588, and in Puebla de los Angeles (Mexico) by 1643.[10] It may well have reached Japan and Puebla *via* Seville. We have had no opportunity to search for it in the sixteenth century, but at least six Seville printers used it between 1617 and 1678. An alternative to Guyot's was Tavernier's *ascendonica romaine*. It is not common anywhere in Spain (though found in Lisbon as early as 1569), but Gerónimo de Contreras and Gabriel Ramos Vejarano had it in 1619. Contreras also had the largest typeface attributable to Guyot, his *canon*, which we have never seen in Madrid, though it is found in Lisbon, in Coimbra, and in the work of several printers of the Seville area.[11] Finally, one typeface offers circumstantial evidence which is almost conclusive: Granjon's *ascendonica cursive*, 'Flemish' by virtue of the fact that the original punches and the four sets of strikes, only one of them justified for casting, were all owned by the Plantin-Moretus house in Antwerp (as they still are). This typeface is very rare outside the work of the Plantin-Moretus firm, but we have found it in

[10] Vervliet, pp. 286–7, 268, 248–9. Some of these occurrences were noted by Vervliet, others in our own investigations.

[11] Vervliet, pp. 246–7, 228–9. We have not seen the eccentric lower-case z of the original Tavernier *ascendonica* used in Spain (see, for example, Alonso de Herrera, *Discursos predicables*, Contreras, 1619, and Fernando de Herrera, *Versos*, Ramos Vejarano, 1619).

Seville as early as the 1630s.[12] It was still in use there in the 1680s, and we shall discuss it again in that context. We shall also show that other types from the Low Countries, especially Dutch ones, are associated with Seville printing in the later seventeenth century. By the eighteenth century the printer Joseph Navarro y Armijo was boasting in an imprint that his products were printed 'en la Imprenta de Caractères de Antuerpia'.[13] Navarro printed from about 1736 to 1759, but we have not checked how often he used this imprint, nor with what degree of justification. Not all printers were so keen to admit to using imported material, though his boast could probably have been made at any time during the previous two centuries.

The decline of Spanish typefounding is not peculiar to Seville. What is perhaps peculiar is that Seville, by far the largest city in Spain (an estimated 160,000 by the end of the sixteenth century), imported type from Madrid, then only a quarter of Seville's size. Other signs of decline, such as wretched paper, poorer ink, inferior presswork, and, finally, lower output, also manifested themselves throughout Spain, but not always simultaneously, so it seems that local conditions played a part. For example, Valladolid produced as many printed items in the five-year period 1601–5 as it did in any subsequent decade of the seventeenth century, simply because Valladolid was the capital of Spain from 1601 to 1606. Medina del Campo, the site of an important international fair in medieval times, declined steadily as a commercial centre in the course of the sixteenth century. Printing still flourished there in the middle

[12] J. Dreyfus (ed.), *Type specimen facsimiles II,* London, 1972, no. 17, item 10 (notes, p. 8); Carter and Vervliet had seen it only in the work of the Plantin-Moretus house. The Plantin firm is known to have cast type for Spanish and Portuguese customers in 1735–41 (L. Voet, *The Golden Compasses*, Amsterdam, 1969–72, 2 vols., ii, 125, n. 4); it must have been doing so at least a century earlier.

[13] See Santiago Montoto, *Impresos sevillanos*, Madrid, 1948, no. 359, and plate facing p. 142. Further references to Montoto will give his name and the item number.

of the century, but by 1609 had ceased entirely, to begin again only in the nineteenth century.

The barometers of Seville's prosperity were the silver imports and the Indies trade, the latter to a large extent financed by the former. Silver imports reached their height (over 42,000,000 ducats) in the years 1591–5, while trade began to decline early in the seventeenth century. The high point came in 1608, when 45,000 tons of shipping sailed from Seville, but Professor J. H. Elliott has named 1622 as marking the start of a period of serious decline.[14] Perhaps it is significant that the period 1621–5 marks the first important drop in Seville's book production in over a century: just over 130 dated items, compared with almost 170 in the previous five-year period.[15]

By the 1620s Seville's population had already begun to decline, and another indication of the printers' difficulties had begun to be more obvious: piracy. Piracy had never been wholly absent, even in prosperous times, when it had been a means of earning even more money. Now it became a means of survival, and received an unhealthy impetus from two sources. One was the writings of Lope de Vega in particular, the other the government ban on the printing of novels and plays in Castile, a ban which lasted from 1625 until 1634. The *Tercera parte de las comedias de Lope de Vega y otros auctores*, 'Barcelona, Sebastian Cormellas' [but Seville, Gabriel Ramos Vejarano] of 1612 was one of the first Lope piracies, but once the ban had been imposed in far-off Madrid, a veritable flood of material with false imprints and dates issued from Seville presses. The quantity involved is only just beginning to im-

[14] J. H. Elliott, *Imperial Spain 1469–1716*, London, 1963, p. 175.

[15] See D. W. Cruickshank, '"Literature" and the book trade in Golden-Age Spain', *MLR*, lxxiii (1978), p. 802. These figures are from Escudero, who seriously under-records; but the extent to which he does so is probably about the same for two successive five-year periods. Escudero can be supplemented from Gestoso y Pérez (note 5), Montoto (note 13), F. Aguilar Piñal, 'Relaciones impresas en Sevilla en el siglo XVII', *Revista de Literatura*, xxxii (1967), 105–30, and from such catalogues as have printer-indexes (e.g. Penney, note 29 below).

pinge on bibliographers, despite the fact that Seville soon acquired the reputation of being a den of piracy in contemporary Spain, and retained it throughout the seventeenth century.[16] Output for the early years of the ban, i.e. 1626–30, ostensibly fell to just half of what it had been a decade earlier, but there is good reason to believe that the collapse was less disastrous than the figures for dated books would suggest.

Piracy, however, was not what annoyed authors most, since the majority of them earned little from printing their works in any case: it was the fact that printers turned out the work of inferior writers under the major authors' names, thereby improving sales. Thus Lope de Vega, after a lifetime of such treatment, wryly assured readers of his *El castigo sin venganza* (Barcelona, 1634) that they could safely regard it as his, since it was *not* printed in Seville; while Don Juan de Vera Tassis, Calderón's friend and editor, said in 1682 that he had heard that almost all the plays printed in Seville for the Indies market were attributed to Calderón.[17] 'Almost all' is an exaggeration, but, as we shall see, it is based on the truth.

The desperate plight of Seville printers in the early twenties, just before the ban, was mentioned in a petition by Juan Serrano de Vargas, a Seville printer who must have been something of a saint, unless he was a thwarted sinner. He described the deplorably pernicious works entering Spain from abroad, and claimed that the Spanish printers would turn out even worse material, if it were not for the restraining influence of the Inquisition, so desperate were they for work. He said that there was work enough for thirteen or fourteen master printers in

[16] See J. Moll, 'La "Tercera parte de las comedias de Lope de Vega y otros auctores", falsificación sevillana', *Revista de Archivos, Bibliotecas y Museos*, lxxvii (1974), 619–26; for the ban, see his 'Diez años sin licencias para imprimir comedias y novelas en los reinos de Castilla: 1625–1634', *Boletín de la Real Academia Española*, liv (1974), 97–103.

[17] For the Lope *suelta* of *El castigo sin venganza*, see Chapter IV below (especially note 32); and Don Pedro Calderón de la Barca, *Verdadera quinta parte de comedias*, Madrid, 1682, ¶¶1r.

Castile (including Andalusia), whereas the actual number trying to make a living was forty-seven.[18]

The ban was never officially revoked: it simply fell into desuetude, probably because the authorities realised that it was unenforceable. The end of the ban, however, produced no sudden upsurge in the quantity of dated items turned out by Seville presses, probably because the nature of that output had been gradually changing. Thirty-five of the 203 known items printed by Cromberger between 1503 and the end of 1520, or almost exactly a sixth, were verse chap-books. Slightly over half of his total output consisted of items with ten sheets or less (no exact figure can be given here, since the collation of lost or fragmentary work is not known). As we shall see presently, the proportion of ephemeral (or merely flimsy) material rose considerably in the course of the next century and a half, to reach very nearly three quarters of the total output of Seville printers. As one of us has tried to show elsewhere, this was partly a reflection of the printers' increasing shortage of capital for long-term investment, partly a reflection of public demand, which the printers both stimulated and relied on.[19]

The ban on the printing of novels and plays was not the only ineffective government measure. In 1627 the ban was reiterated in a decree which also attempted to control the printing of

[18] M. Agulló y Cobo, 'La inquisición y los libreros españoles en el siglo XVII', *Cuadernos bibliográficos*, 28, Madrid, 1972, p. 147.

[19] See note 15, Cruickshank, '"Literature" and the book trade . . .'. Inevitably, some large books had to be printed outside Spain. When François Bertaut visited Father Antonio de Escobar y Mendoza in the course of his travels in Spain in 1659–60, he recalled their conversation thus: 'Comme il n'avoit pas veu ces Lettres dont je viens de parler [Pascal's *Lettres provinciales*], je luy promis de luy en envoyer de France, & de parler aux Libraires de Lyon qui impriment ses oeuvres, & dont il n'estoit pas satisfait: car il n'y a point d'Imprimeurs en Espagne assez forts pour entreprendre de grands Ouvrages, qu'ils envoyent tous imprimer à Lyon ou à Anvers. Il me dit qu'ils luy imprimoient huit Tomes *in-folio* de sa Theologie Morale' [*Universae theologiae moralis*, Lyon, 1652–63, ten folio volumes, eight of them presumably printed by 1659]: [F. Bertaut], *Journal du voyage d'Espagne*, Paris, 1682, pp. 194–5.

ephemera in particular; the attempt had no impact. In 1634 a tax was imposed on printed matter: it was repealed in two years after vehement protests. But if the government had little influence, other factors had: in 1649 Seville was ravaged by the plague, and half the population is said to have perished. As so often happens in such cases, 'half' is probably an overestimate; and although two very active printers, Francisco de Lyra Barreto and Pedro Gómez de Pastrana, printed their last works in 1648 and 1649 respectively, there is no proof that this is anything but a coincidence. On the other hand, there is no doubt that the commercial life of the city, including, inevitably, the book trade, suffered a further serious setback. The output of dated books, which had risen in the period 1641–5, showed two successive declines in the periods 1646–50 and 1651–5.

★ ★ ★ ★ ★ ★

Some of the previous paragraphs have implied that Seville books are quite distinctive, being printed in a wide range of types, a few of them found nowhere else in Spain. This is true to a degree, except that Seville printers who bought their cast type in Madrid naturally tended to produce work which can be confused with Madrid printing. Moreover, the demand for typographical material in Seville was such that it seems sometimes to have been shared, and invariably to have been taken over by one printer from another. As a result, successive printers in Seville often had similar stocks of type. To find differences, the investigator must look for wear, damage and adulteration. Thanks, no doubt, to the somewhat desperate straits of the printers, all of these are quite common.

In the course of this investigation we have examined about 400 Seville items, half of them printed between 1670 and 1683, the period covered by the forty-two dated items in Pepys 1545. The majority of the remainder were printed between 1620 and 1670. Many of these items were chap-books or pamphlets: those in Pepys 1545 and, in particular, three volumes of pamphlets in the British Library, pressmarks 1445.f.17, 811.e.51

and 593.h.17. The last of these is a collection of well over a hundred pamphlets printed in Seville between 1623 and 1639 and collected by Don Andrés Fernández de León y Ledesma; while it provided no direct evidence for the Pepys material, it supplied much useful information about Seville printing in the earlier seventeenth century.

We have also compiled a checklist of items produced by the printers who were active in Seville in the second half of the seventeenth century, with a view to discovering as much as possible about the subject-matter and quantity of their output. This checklist comprises over 400 items, of which we have seen about half. The phrase 'printers who were active' conceals a multitude of difficulties. We know that it was the practice in Seville (and elsewhere in Spain) for printing-house foremen to use their names in imprints. If, as sometimes happened, the proprietor's name was used in other imprints, we can be deceived as to the actual number of firms in operation. Occasionally an imprint tells us (nearly) all. The most tantalising in this respect are those found on the broadsides produced to celebrate the reputed martyrdom (6 May) of St John the Evangelist, to whom Spanish printers were particularly devoted. Montoto (item 197) describes eight of these and illustrates one: all are of 1674. The printers would set up an elaborate design of type, flowers and other ornaments to accompany verses, which they seem also to have composed. The individual workmen made their own sheets, and gave the name of the press where they were printed, thus:

> En la imprenta de la viuda de Nicolas Rodriguez de Abrego, 1674. Clemente Rey.
>
> Impresso en la imprenta de la viuda de Nicolas Rodriguez. Juan Antonio Tarazona.

This suggests that Rey and Tarazona, whom we shall meet again later, worked in the press of the widow Rodríguez in 1674. By the same token, we may suppose that Francisco Carlos de Paredes, Francisco de Mazinas and Gabriel Gutiérrez were all employed by J. F. de Blas; we shall not hear of them again. One item links Manuel Ramos with Blas, but another, with verses written by Tomé de Dios Miranda and embellished with a block cut by him, is said to be printed by the same Ramos. Who was working for whom? Only typographical analysis can hope to give an answer, but we have not seen this sheet.

The most important printing family in Seville during this period was that of Blas. The father of the firm was Juan Gómez de Blas, who began printing in 1633, and who eventually acquired the title of 'impresor mayor' of Seville, the first printer to do so.[20] In practice, this meant that he produced some 'official' ephemera, but he also printed, for example, Juan de Esquivel Navarro's prized book on dance, the *Discursos sobre el arte del dançado* of 1642. Beginning in 1661, and probably following the example set in Madrid, he was the first Seville printer to produce a periodical *Gaceta* (see Montoto 176–87 for the first twelve numbers). None of the Pepys chap-books or plays was produced by him, but Pepys had a copy of his 1664 edition of Cervantes's *Novelas exemplares* (Gaselee 37); he also had one of the last items produced by Juan Gómez, the *Fiestas que celebro la iglesia parrochial de S. Maria la Blanca* of 1666 (Gaselee 63). Juan Gómez is known to have printed one item in 1667. He sometimes added an address to his imprints, 'by the College of San Acacio', which was apparently in the Calle de la Sierpe (see below). About 1660 the firm moved to the Calle de Génova which, as we have seen, was the address of Ungut and Polono in 1491.

If we accept Escudero's item 1699 at its face value, Juan Gómez's son Juan Francisco first used his name in an imprint in 1662. His name does not appear again until 1667, when he used the title 'impresor mayor', so it seems likely that he took over the firm in the latter year, and ran it until 1722, when the name of his son Juan Francisco de Blas y Quesada appears for

[20] See Escudero, pp. 42, 43, 47, 49. For a more up-to-date account of the family, see F. Aguilar Piñal's 'El impresor mayor de la ciudad', *Temas sevillanos*, i, Seville, 1972, 15–21, and his *Impresos sevillanos del siglo XVIII*, Madrid, 1974, pp. 12–13.

the first time. Another son, Florencio Joseph de Blas y Quesada, reprinted in 1748 Melchor de Cabrera's book in praise of printing, which had first appeared in 1675. No doubt he was familiar with the passage on folio 22^{r} of the 1675 edition, where his father and grandfather are mentioned: 'La Ciudad de Sevilla diò à Iuan Gomez de Blâs el titulo de su Impressor Mayor, con el goze de trezientos ducados de gages en cada vn año, de los dos Cabildos, Eclesiastico, y Seglar, del Santo Tribunal de la Inquisicion, y de la Vniversidad, y Colegio Mayor; y oy se continua esta gracia en Iuan Francisco de Blàs su hijo'.[21] This evidently means that the various bodies mentioned together guaranteed the Blas family an annual income of 300 ducats, a not insubstantial sum.

Between 1667 and 1700 Juan Francisco de Blas printed eighty-two signed items that we know of. Since sixty of these, or nearly three quarters, comprise ten sheets or less, we must assume that much of his output is lost or unrecorded: an 'impresor mayor' could scarcely have justified his guaranteed income on the basis of only five items every two years, especially when many of those items were rather flimsy. Thirty-nine items, or nearly half of the total, could be classified loosely as 'religious'; twenty-two items, or over a quarter, are 'accounts of events', i.e. news. All of the news items are ephemeral. The remaining twenty-one items include medicine (five: Seville University still had an active medical faculty), government publications (four), law (three), grammar (three), and six miscellaneous items. These last six include two of his most notable pieces of work: Joseph de Veitia Linage's *Norte de la contratacion de las Yndias Occidentales* of 1671 (or 1672), a massive folio (Escudero 1738); and Antonio de Gastañeta Iturrivalzaga's *Norte de la navegacion, hallado por el quadrante de la reduccion* of 1692, another big folio (Escudero 1885). Given Pepys's interest

21 M. de Cabrera Núñez de Guzmán, *Discurso legal, historico, y politico, en prueba del origen, progresos, utilidad, nobleza, y excelencias del arte de la imprenta*, Madrid, 1675, fol. 22^{r}. For the Seville 1748 edition, see Montoto 358.

in his job in the Admiralty, it is not surprising that he had a copy of the Veitia Linage (now Pepys 2159, Gaselee 180, the 1672 issue). No doubt he would have bought the other had it been available when he was in Seville in 1684.

The contract for one of Juan Francisco de Blas's books has been preserved. It states that Juan Francisco, son of Juan Gómez de Blas and Magdalena de Solís, resident in the Calle de Génova, agreed to print Juan de Aguilar Camacho's *Catecismo predicable* (Escudero 1768) in *atanasia* (english), on Genoa paper. There were to be 400 copies, the charge was five ducats per sheet, and the completion date was to be ten months from 5 October 1673 (the book is actually dated 1675).[22] Since the book is a quarto of seventy-five sheets, Blas must have been paid 375 ducats for printing the 400 copies. The standard retail price of a Spanish book was by then six *maravedís* a sheet, or 450 *maravedís* for a book of seventy-five sheets. Since Blas had been paid almost exactly 328 *maravedís* per copy (reckoning at the Castilian rate of 350 *maravedís* per ducat), the bookseller's gross profit would have been about 122 *maravedís* per copy, or, in the unlikely event of his selling all 400, nearly 140 ducats, which is just over twenty-seven per cent. Payment to the author and the giving of complimentary copies to the licensing authorities would have reduced this considerably.[23] Three quarters of a century earlier, 122 *maravedís* would have rated 1/9d at par, but by 1675 it was probably little more than a shilling (the wage of a Castilian labourer in 1600 was 170 *maravedís* a week; by 1650 it was 250 *maravedís*, although in real terms this was, if anything, a decrease).

In 1678 (or in 1679, according to Escudero 1800) a book appeared with the imprint of 'the heirs of Juan Gómez de Blas'. We do not know whether this was a new name or a new firm; in either case, it was short-lived. As for Lorenzo Ortiz's

[22] Gestoso y Pérez, *Noticias inéditas*, p. 149.

[23] J. M. Blecua, 'Dos memoriales de libreros a Felipe IV', *Homenaje a Casalduero*, Madrid, 1972, pp. 97, 99, quotes booksellers' complaints at losses caused by these 'gifts' of complimentary copies.

Origen y instituto de la compañia de Jesus, which was printed for Juan Salvador Pérez 'in the College of San Hermenegildo' in 1679, it is typographically similar to the work of Juan Francisco de Blas, but we are not wholly convinced that he was the printer. There is evidence that the college had its own press which was operated for it by a succession of master printers who had establishments of their own (see Escudero 806, 869, and p. 34). There is also evidence that the college had some type of its own, so typographical evidence cannot identify the printer positively. Finally, there is a newsletter recorded by Simón Díaz as having been printed in Seville in 1676 by 'Juan de Quesada'.[24] Without claiming that the date was printed or has been recorded incorrectly, we suggest that this name conceals that of Juan [Francisco] de [Blas y] Quesada, who apparently succeeded his father in 1722, but who may well have been alive, and perhaps even in charge of the firm long before this date, without bothering to add his mother's surname, Quesada, to that of his father.

The next major printer to concern us, in chronological order, is Nicolás Rodríguez de Abrego, who worked in the Calle de Génova from 1638 onwards. His was one of at least two printing-houses in that street, for Andrés Grande (active 1624–50) also gave the Calle de Génova as his address. We shall discuss this address at greater length later. Between 1667 and 1671 (the exact year is unknown, for no dated items are recorded for the period 1668–70), Rodríguez died and was succeeded by his widow, who printed until 1674. We know of only thirty-nine items produced by Rodríguez and his widow, an average of only one a year, and since twenty-six have ten sheets or fewer, this figure must give an underestimate of true output. As with the Blas family, nearly half of the Rodríguez firm's output can be classified under 'religion', and again 'news' comes second, this time with a third. The only significant difference is that 'literature', with five items, comes next,

[24] J. Simón Díaz, *Impresos del siglo XVII*, Madrid, 1972, no. 1368.

followed by law (two items) and medicine (one). The literature included Juan Pérez de Montalbán's *Sucessos y prodigios de amor en ocho novelas exemplares* (1641), and a reprint of the Hoces edition of Góngora's *Todas las obras* (1648). (Pepys had an edition of the former printed in Cadiz by Bartolomé Núñez de Castro, probably in 1682 – Gaselee 134.) Curiously enough, we know of fourteen signed items printed by the widow Rodríguez in the years 1671–4. Thus over a third of the firm's recorded production falls in the last four years of its existence. Perhaps even more curiously, there are signs of a change in policy: twelve of the widow's fourteen items are undeniably 'religion', while the two we have classified as 'news' are, first, an account of how the Jesuits in Seville converted forty-four Turks and Moors, of whom thirty-eight were baptised by the Archbishop of Seville, and second, an account sent home from the Philippines by a Spanish missionary. The widow's piety seems to have borne fruit, for apart from apparently printing more, she also printed larger and more magnificent books than her husband had ever done. The best-known of these is Fernando de la Torre Farfán's *Fiestas de la S. Yglesia Metropolitana, y Patriarcal de Sevilla*, a handsome coffee-table folio of about ninety sheets, not counting the many plates, one of them drawn by Murillo himself and engraved by the Sevillian craftsman Arteaga (Escudero 1736). Readers of Pepys will remember that he was particularly fond of engravings. Also, in his list of the things he wanted to see in Seville was 'Morello's [i.e. Murillo's] paintings at a house of disabled people where we are to go'.[25] These two interests no doubt explain why he bought a copy of the book; it is now Pepys 2144 (Gaselee 172).

[25] See his instructions to his nephew John Jackson regarding the purchase of religious prints in Spain in *Private correspondence and miscellaneous papers of Samuel Pepys*, ed. J. R. Tanner, London, 1926, 2 vols., ii, 3–4. His 'see' list is reproduced by E. M. Wilson in *Transactions of the Cambridge Bibliographical Society*, II, ii (1955), facing p. 130. We thank Mr R. Latham for deciphering the shorthand for us (only the word 'Morello's' is not in shorthand).

Less well-known and splendid, but over twice as big (nearly 200 sheets) is her folio edition of the *Constituciones synodales del obispado de Malaga* of 1674 (Escudero 1755). What is odd about all this is that Nicolás Rodríguez is known to have printed only one folio, and that of three sheets; his most ambitious work appears to have been the Góngora, of sixty-one and a half sheets. Moreover, while Nicolás's presswork is typical Spanish seventeenth-century (that is, poor), his widow's is well above average, even in her chap-book carols. Finally, the widow acted in a modest way as a 'publisher'. Although she printed none of the chap-books in Pepys 1545, number 17/49, printed by Tomé de Dios Miranda with no date, appeared 'a costa de la viuda de Nicolas Rodriguez, y vendese en su casa en call [*sic*] de Genova'. The cost of numbers 38/158 and 64/40, both printed by Miranda in 1675, was also met by her, and it was stated that the items were available on her premises, though no address was given. Perhaps the profits from her large folios enabled her to take this step; in any event, the chap-books show that she was still active in the book trade the year after the date of her last known book. One would like to know whether the widow or a new foreman was responsible for the change in policy, and for the improvements in standards and output; but we can only guess. If we are to believe the St John broadsides, the widow had Clemente Rey and Juan Antonio Tarazona among her employees at this time. Both were accomplished printers, and Tarazona seems to have been running a press in Jerez during this period as well (for the widow, or independently?). No doubt she produced the two folios under contract (i.e. she was merely paid for printing: others bore the cost and possible financial loss of publishing). Even so, the fact remains that her husband had been unable to secure any such contracts.

Juan de Ossuna, who gave his address as 'a la esquina de la Cárcel Real', at the corner of the Royal Prison, was not the first printer to occupy his premises. Bartolomé Gómez de Pastrana and his successor (son?) Pedro Gómez de Pastrana had worked there from 1603 to 1649. If this firm *was* one of the casualties of the plague of 1649, the possibility may explain why Ossuna's first book is dated 1652: the plague also interrupted continuity. From the trading viewpoint at least the premises would appear to have been very desirable; Alonso Morgado's *Historia de Sevilla* (1587) describes the site thus: 'One should make a point of seeing the Royal Prison at the entrance to the Calle de la Sierpe. It has a character all its own; it is very easy for foreigners to find because of the endless flow of people at all hours of the day in and out of the main gate, as well as the inscriptions of the gate, which is emblazoned with both the arms of the king and the arms of Seville.'[26] The Calle de la Sierpe was one of the best known of Seville's streets, although not always for the best reasons, as the references to it in *El burlador de Sevilla* by Don Juan and his friend make clear. It also had a long association with printers and booksellers, so it seems quite possible that Ossuna's shop was on the Sierpe corner in particular. We are not certain that Ossuna was still in business when Pepys visited Seville, although he bought nine items with his imprint; but it is perhaps worth remarking that one of the places listed in Pepys's Tangier papers for visiting is the 'prison and workhouse'.[27] The prison is also noteworthy in that part of *Don Quixote* was written in it.

Ossuna signed his books intermittently with the name Juan Méndez de Ossuna between 1656 and 1662. One item (Montoto 148) gives his title as 'Impressor mayor de los Colegios, y Estudios'. According to Escudero, he did not print after 1674, but six of the chap-books in Pepys 1545 were printed by

[26] Quoted by M. Defourneaux, *Daily life in Spain in the Golden Age*, London, 1970, p. 89. See also B. J. Gallardo, *Ensayo para una biblioteca de libros raros y curiosos*, Madrid, 1863–89, 4 vols., i, cols. 1341–70, and the *Entremés de la cárcel de Sevilla*, ibid., cols. 1372–84. The *entremés* was edited by Dámaso Alonso in *El hospital de los podridos y otros entremeses alguna vez atribuidos a Cervantes*, Madrid, 1936.

[27] See note 25 above, and also W. Matthews, 'Samuel Pepys and Spain', *Neophilologus*, xx (1935), 120–9.

him between 1677 and 1681. Several of these late items carry the legend 'Y se vende en su casa', that is, they were for sale on his premises. Both Simón Díaz and Palau, apparently independently, quote one item printed as late as 1687. We have not seen a copy, and we are not wholly convinced that the date is accurate.[28] If it is, it must mean that Ossuna concentrated less on printing and more on bookselling towards the end of his career.

During his thirty years of activity (including the 1687 item but not accepting the date) Ossuna printed only twenty-four items that we know of. Two-thirds of them had ten leaves or fewer. All eight of the larger items, and six of the others, deal with religion (well over half). 'Popular literature' accounts for six items (by 'popular literature' we mean two things: work that deserves to be called 'popular' rather than 'literary', and the work of serious authors in a format suitable for popular consumption). Finally there are four items of 'news'.

Unlike the Rodríguez firm, which apparently became more prosperous towards the end of its existence, Ossuna's production appears to have consisted of progressively more small items (although it is probably unwise to form any conclusions about so little material). During the period 1652–62 the eight known items run to 265, $25\frac{1}{4}$, $\frac{1}{2}$, $\frac{1}{2}$, 1, 2, $36\frac{1}{2}$ and 58 sheets respectively. There is then a huge gap until 1671, after which over half his output consists of one-sheet chap-books. However, since the 'over half' is in reality the nine items saved for us by Pepys, these figures are somewhat misleading. On the other hand, none of his later work approaches the size of the huge *Chronica de la Provincia de San Gabriel*, by Fray Juan de la Trinidad, a folio of well over 1000 pages, which he printed in 1652. This was certainly produced under contract, and it would seem that he never got such a contract again. Two of his ventures into the field of popular literature involved drama

[28] Simón Díaz, *Impresos*, no. 1082; A. Palau y Dulcet, *Manual del librero hispano-americano*, Barcelona, 1948– , no. 347011.

(Pepys 1545, 43/174 and 45/113, of 1673 and 1681). The first consists of four *loas* (short dramatic pieces designed as prologues for longer works), the second of two extracts – more or less complete in themselves – from plays by Cristóbal de Monroy and Juan Pérez de Montalbán.

Before turning to Tomé de Dios Miranda, the next printer whose work is particularly relevant to this study, we shall deal briefly with several printers or supposed printers who were active in Seville in the 1650s and 1660s. Their work is not directly relevant, but a glance at their activities helps to throw some light on the general situation of the book trade in Seville at this time.

According to Escudero (no. 1647), the *Ynstruccion de novicios de la Orden de Descalços*, an anonymous work of 1651, bears the legend 'En Sevilla, por Juan Lorenzo Bispo'. We have no reason to associate the surname Bispo with printing anywhere in Spain, and in view of the coincidence in Christian names and in dates, we suspect that this printer is connected with, and probably to be identified with Juan Lorenzo Machado, whose handful of imprints covers the years 1653–60. If the two men are the same, then Machado's career begins two years earlier than was previously supposed. In any event Bispo was apparently a printer and not, as Escudero suggests, a bookseller or publisher. If he is to be identified with Machado, the most likely explanation for the two surnames is that they were maternal and paternal ones. His last known item (1660 – Montoto 160) gives his address as 'Enfrente de la Carcel de la Real Audiencia'.

Under item 1227 of his *Impresos del siglo XVII*, Simón Díaz cites a newsletter concerning the conversion to Catholicism of the Queen of Sweden (1654), and gives the printer as Francisco Ignacio. Escudero gives no help with this name, but under entries 1648 and 1654 (dated 1651 and 1653), he describes items printed by Francisco Ygnacio de Lyra. This name does not appear in his preliminary list of printers, but that it is no error is confirmed by the presence in the British Library of another copy of the second item (Francisco Duarte de Tavora's

Copia de un parecer . . . acerca del uso de las samgrias [sic] *del tovillo*, 783.g.21[3]). Two more items, one in the British Library and one in the collection of the Hispanic Society of America, are printed 'Apud Ignatium de Lyra, 1653'. This is almost certainly the same person, a relative (probably a son) of the more famous Seville printer Francisco de Lyra Barreto (or Lira Varreto), whose last known work is dated 1648, as we said earlier. If Francisco Ignacio succeeded Francisco, the plague of 1649 might explain the apparent hiatus (1648–51) and the fact that Francisco Ignacio's products are rather more modest than Francisco's.

Escudero's item 1659, the *Catenae moralis doctrinae tractatum* of Pedro de Tapia (1654), is somewhat puzzling. It is a folio of not much less than 200 sheets (i.e. it would have taken some time, probably months, to print) and it is signed 'Hispali. Apud *Salvatorem de Cea Teza*'. Salvador de Cea Teza (or Tesa) was the most active printer in Córdoba during the period 1620–65. We have no reason to believe that he moved all his equipment temporarily to Seville to print this book. Perhaps he was brought in to supervise its printing on some other press, as seems to have been the practice with the press of the College of San Hermenegildo (see above). The second volume of the work was printed three years later, under unexceptional circumstances, by Juan Gómez de Blas.

Escudero records that between 1657 and 1659 a certain Juan de Ribera printed three Latin works in Seville. A person of this name printed in Mexico City from 1677 to 1684, and his widow until 1700. If this is another émigré from Seville, he is only one of a number of Seville printers who came to the conclusion that they could make a better living elsewhere.

In 1664 Pedro de la Fuente's *Passo riguroso del Jordan de la muerte*, a substantial folio, appeared with the imprint of Clemente Rey, 'En la casa grande de S. Francisco' (Escudero 1705). Clemente may well have been related to Fernando Rey, who printed in Seville from 1615 to 1617, and later in Jerez, San Lúcar and Cadiz (until at least 1646). Clemente certainly had a longer career than the one signed item implies: in 1674 he was apparently working for the widow Rodríguez, as we said above. Perhaps he spent some of his earlier career as printer to the monastery of St Francis. There is some reason to believe that several of the larger religious houses kept a press on their premises for their private use, only occasionally producing work which was publicly disseminated.

Also in 1664 there appeared José Román de la Torre y Peralta's *Festin de las tres gracias*, a quarto pamphlet with the imprint of Miguel de Aldabe. Miss Penney describes a copy belonging to the Hispanic Society of America;[29] Simón Díaz (*Impresos del siglo XVII*, no. 241) lists other copies in the Biblioteca Nacional, Madrid. The only other record of this printer is in a quarto newsletter of two leaves (Montoto 120), which is signed 'Miguel de Aldabe, en la calle de la Sierpe, junto al Colegio de San Acacio', and dated 1653. 'By the College of San Acacio' was then the address of Juan Gómez de Blas. If Aldabe was a foreman or one of the journeymen employed by Blas, it would explain how he apparently survived for eleven years on two pieces of ephemera.

In 1666 an edition of Antonio Hurtado de Mendoza's *Vida de Nuestra Señora* was printed in Seville by Lucas Antonio de Bedmar; it is a slim octavo (Montoto 191). The following year Bedmar printed the proceedings of a literary academy which took place on February 17th; this is a quarto of twelve sheets (see Escudero 1719 and 1721). Bedmar gave his address as the Calle de Génova. By 1669 he was in Madrid, 'beside the Fuente de los Relatores', where he had a long and apparently successful career as a printer, being succeeded by his son, who printed well into the eighteenth century. At one stage he and some of his Madrid colleagues had a dispute with a group of beggars who made a meagre living by selling printed ephemeral matter in the streets. One of the angry beggars called him a

[29] C. L. Penney, *List of books printed 1601–1700 in the Library of the Hispanic Society of America*, New York, 1938, p. 633.

'perro morisco andaluz', which indicates that he came from the south of Spain (perhaps Seville itself: his accent probably gave him away), and possibly that his complexion was somewhat swarthy, as is the case with many Andalusians today.[30] Although Bedmar's output in Madrid includes a great deal of the sort of material sold by the beggars, many of his books were substantial, and he eventually achieved the distinction of becoming a royal printer. Some indication of his prosperity may be deduced from the fact that shortly after his arrival in Madrid, the town council of Antequera (in Andalusia, near Málaga) tried to persuade him to move to that city, offering to give him a house and an annual income of a hundred ducats and two *cahices* (38 bushels) of wheat. He elected to remain in Madrid, evidently considering that printing in the provinces was less profitable than printing in the capital.[31]

The next printer whose work concerns us closely is Tomé de Dios Miranda. We know of twenty-one items bearing his name, and of three which can be attributed to him: the earliest is dated 1666, the latest 1678. Four of the signed items and two of the attributable ones are in Pepys 1545. After the imprint in Pepys 1545/15/83 the words 'Vendese en calle de Genova' appear, as a separate sentence. As mentioned earlier, Pepys 1545/64/40, 38/158 and 17/49 were printed by Miranda for the widow Rodríguez. The third of these added 'y se vende en su casa en call de Genova', which almost certainly refers to the widow's premises. To these three we can probably add Escudero 1959, an item which bears no imprint except for the statement that it was printed for the widow Rodríguez; it consists of popular literature in ephemeral form, which, as we shall see, is typical of Miranda. The reference to the Calle de Génova in Pepys 1545/15/83 does not necessarily mean that Miranda worked there, especially since the item is dated 1675,

30 C. Espejo, 'Pleito entre ciegos e impresores (1680–1775)', *Revista de la Biblioteca, Archivo y Museo*, ii (1925), 211.

31 Cabrera Núñez de Guzmán, *Discurso* . . ., fol. 22r (see note 21). Bedmar was the printer of the 1675 edition.

by which time he was already printing work to be sold by the widow Rodríguez, who certainly lived in that street.

Pepys 1545/65/77, like Escudero 1959, carries only the name of the person for whom it was printed in 1670 ('. . . en Sevilla, a costa de Iuan de Yllanes, en la calle de Genova'). This is the only record of Juan de Yllanes (or Illanes?). The print contains four woodblocks; two of these were used by Miranda in item 38/158 (1675), and one was used by Cabezas and by Vejarano (54/1 and 40/11, no date and 1682), who are known to have inherited blocks from Miranda. The fourth block, however, and one of the first two appear together in Pepys 1545/63/56, which claims to have been printed 'en Madrid por la Viuda de Melchor Clegre [sic]. Año de 1672', and which was ostensibly sold 'en casa de la Viuda de Iuan de Valdes en frente dè Santo Tomas'.[32] The widows of Melchor Alegre and Juan de Valdés were indeed in business in Madrid at that time, but we do not think they had anything to do with this printing, for a number of reasons: first, we have not seen the battered text-type (*c.* 95 mm/20 lines) in Madrid books, but it is the same as that used in 65/77, said to be printed in Seville for Yllanes; second, while it is not unlikely that two blocks used in Seville in 1670 should turn up in Madrid in 1672, we think it most improbable that one of them should make its way back to Seville in 1675; third, the mistake in the name (Clegre) seems more understandable if we accept that the compositor who made it was working for an entirely different printer. The simplest explanation is that Miranda owned all four of the blocks in question, that he printed 65/77 for Yllanes in 1670, and that he reprinted 63/56 in 1672 from a Madrid edition; the preservation of the original imprint was either a trivial piece of deception for piratical reasons, or the act of a mindless compositor.

If we count the Yllanes and the 'Clegre' items and Escudero

[32] Wilson, 'Samuel Pepys's Spanish chap-books', part 3, pp. 312–13; for a list of recurring blocks, see part 1, pp. 133–5. The four blocks mentioned here are numbers xvi, xvi *bis*, xvii and xviii. The list also shows how other blocks used by Miranda were later used by Cabezas or Vejarano.

1959, Miranda's output comes to twenty-four items, of which fifteen have ten sheets or fewer. If this figure gives the impression that Miranda printed larger works than his contemporaries, the impression is a false one: four of the remaining nine items have between eleven and fifteen sheets, and only three have more than fifty sheets, the largest being Diego Ortiz's *Logicae brevis explicatio* (Escudero 1788), printed in 1678, with fifty-eight and a half sheets. As with all Seville printers of this period, religion (ten items) was the most frequent topic. Less usual, perhaps, is the fact that popular literature comes second with six items. 'News' comes third (three items), and the remainder is made up of single examples of medicine, logic, philosophy, etc.

There is evidence that Miranda exercised another skill of particular importance in the printing trade, that of engraving. Montoto's item 230 has no date or imprint, but his illustration of the title-page (facing p. 90) shows an engraving signed 'Thomas à Deo de Mirãda', a latinized form of his name. Montoto also tells us that one of the St John broadsheets of 1674 is decorated with a woodblock of St John signed by Miranda. Finally, number 1064 of Simón Díaz's *Impresos del siglo XVII*, Fray Joseph de San Esteban's *Vida, y virtudes del Venerable Hermano Fray Juan de la Magdalena* (1662) has a copper engraving signed 'Thomé de Dios'. This must be our Miranda. It suggests that he worked for other printers (in this case the printer was Juan de Ossuna) before setting up his own firm.

One of the few Seville printers of this period whose work has survived in sufficient quantity for it to be statistically significant is Juan Cabezas. There is some confusion about the date of his earliest work. Simón Díaz (*Impresos del siglo XVII*, no. 1306) seems to imply that it was 1672, but since the item in question refers to the Holy Year of 1675, this is an obvious error. We consider another item, ostensibly of 1674, to be possibly suspect, but we know of no fewer than fifteen dated works from 1675. He printed steadily for another six years, producing eighty-six items that we know of, and died or retired in 1681.

Sixty-seven items, or over three quarters, have ten sheets or less. The remaining nineteen, unusually, all deal with religion. Some of them are quite substantial, and he produced them with relative consistency throughout his career, for example: 1675, Juan de Cárdenas's *Historia de la vida y virtudes de la venerable virgen Damiana de las Llagas* (Escudero 1767, 96 sheets); 1676, Luis Ayllón y Quadros's *Elucubrationes Bibliae in vetus ac novum testamentum* (Escudero 1771, 227 sheets); 1678, Sor María de la Antigua's *Desengaño de religiosos* (Escudero 1781, 217 sheets, listed under the name of the editor Pedro de Valbuena); 1681, Francisco Sylvestre's *Discursos morales* [and] . . . *dos sermones* (Escudero 1809, 118 sheets). Overall, Cabezas's work falls into three broad categories: religion, a little more than a third; news, almost exactly a third; and popular literature, a little under a third.

The circumstances under which Cabezas established and operated his firm are of some interest, but difficult to ascertain. In one of his earlier works (Escudero 1774, dated 1676), he gave his address as 'opposite the Cárcel de los Señores'. In that year he printed two items (Pepys 1545/50/19 and 55/150) for Lucas Martín de Hermosilla (or Hermosa), who gave his address in the second as 'Calle de Génova'. From 1677 to 1681, on the other hand, Cabezas gave the Calle de Génova as *his* address, usually adding that his products were for sale on his premises. 'Calle de Génova' may be a new address or a new way of describing the old one; at any rate, there was apparently a change in publishing arrangements. As we shall show later, there is evidence that Cabezas acquired much of the typographical material of the widow Rodríguez. Since the widow seems to have stopped printing in 1674 and is not heard of after 1675, whereas Cabezas possibly started printing in 1674 and certainly by 1675, it seems conceivable that he acquired the widow's premises in the Calle de Génova along with her stock (for all we know, he may even have married her). It has already been proved that Cabezas acquired some of the material of Tomé de Dios Miranda who, as we have pointed out, was printing for the widow in 1675.[33] If Miranda lived in the Calle de Génova, we suggest that his premises or the widow's (perhaps even both, if they were indeed separate) were eventually taken over by Cabezas, as also was their typographical material and, to some extent, their printing/publishing partnership. It should be remembered, however, that Miranda continued to print until at least 1678.

In the latter half of 1681 (to judge from his output of that year, compared with that of previous years) Cabezas stopped printing and was succeeded by Juan Vejarano. Vejarano may have been a descendant of Alfonso Vejarano, who had printed in Seville from about 1554 to 1572, but he had been working in Cadiz, where his name occurs in several items printed in the 1670s; one, dated 1673, states that it was printed by Vejarano 'en casa de Bartolomé Núñez' (Penney, p. 4). El Alférez (a military title) Bartolomé Núñez de Castro, to give his full name, printed in Cadiz from the 1670s until the late 1680s, perhaps the early 1690s; Pepys bought at least two items which came from his press.[34] Vejarano was probably Núñez's foreman. As such, he could hardly be expected to have the capital to take over Cabezas's apparently flourishing concern by himself, and this is borne out by the style of his imprints: although he describes himself as an 'Impressor de libros en calle de Genova', all (save one, and possibly another which we have not seen) of his signed pieces of work were printed for Lucas Martín de Hermosilla. There are twenty-nine of these, and they cover the

33 See previous note.

34 One item was Pérez de Montalbán's *Novelas exemplares* (Gaselee 134, see above, p. 20); another was Martín de Velasco's *Arte de sermones* of 1677 (Gaselee 181 – it may be remembered that Pepys at one time compared the sermons of a series of eleven preachers to assess their fitness for naval chaplaincies: see A. Bryant, *Samuel Pepys*, Cambridge, 1932–8, 3 vols., ii, 184–5). Two more items (Pepys 1545/26/23 and 28/25) are carols sung in Cadiz cathedral in December 1683. The first carries the mysterious initials E.C.C.L.: P.E.A.B.N.D.C. The second group of letters almost certainly stands for '*P*or *E*l *A*lférez *B*artolomé *N*úñez *D*e *C*astro', the first perhaps for '*E*n *C*ádiz, *C*iudad *L*eal' or '*E*n *C*ádiz, *C*alle *L* . . .' (i.e. an address). See Wilson, 'Samuel Pepys's Spanish chap-books', part 2, pp. 242–4.

years 1681–3. Twenty-five of them consist of a single sheet; the largest, of twenty-six sheets. The content is approximately two-thirds popular literature to one-third religion, although these figures certainly reflect the tastes of Pepys as a collector of ephemera. It may well be that Lucas Martín de Hermosilla acquired the major share, if not all, of Cabezas's firm. Vejarano may have become his foreman, or at least his tenant, and if he owned the material with which he printed, he was financially dependent upon Hermosilla. He did not try, or was unable to emulate Cabezas's output. After Vejarano had gone, Hermosilla turned to printing on his own account, although apparently not until 1684 (there is one minor work of that year [Montoto 214], another of 1685, followed in 1686 by a two-volumed folio of the works of Father Nieremberg, with a total of 388 sheets in all, which must have taken well over a year to print and so may explain the delay).

Vejarano is of interest because his brief period of activity immediately precedes Pepys's stay in Seville. We can therefore expect his wares to have been more readily available in the shops. This expectation seems to be supported by the fact that Pepys bought twenty-six items with his imprint, a large amount considering the printer's modest output and short working life. Of this total, thirteen are otherwise unknown, a figure which shows only too clearly how the ephemeral products of such printers can vanish without trace unless they are collected and preserved in the first few years of their existence.

The last major printer to concern us here is Tomás López de Haro. López de Haro began printing in 1678, giving his address as the 'Calle de las Siete Revueltas', often adding 'Junto a la Imagen' (this would have been a religious image). Two items dated 1690 and 1707 give the address 'enfrente del Buen Suceso'. Rather than a second set of premises, we think this means that the image in question was of Nuestra Señora del Buen Suceso. By 1682 (Escudero 1813) he was calling himself a *mercader de libros*, literally, a book-merchant; this may mean that he sold wholesale and retail. In 1695 there appeared two flimsy items with the imprint of 'the heirs of Tomás López de Haro', but there is also a slightly more substantial work dated 1696 (Escudero 1918) and signed by Tomás himself. If this is at all significant, it must mean that he died in late 1695. The name of Tomás's heirs continued to appear in imprints until 1718, when one of them, Diego López de Haro, seems to have taken charge. Diego moved to the Calle de Génova about 1720 and printed there until 1752, his widow until 1760.[35] Two items printed by Diego have been incorrectly described as belonging to the seventeenth century. One is Escudero 1963, assigned to the second third of the seventeenth century, despite the name Diego and the address Calle de Génova; the other is a chap-book ballad (no. 260 in Simón Díaz's *Impresos del siglo XVII*).

We know of ninety-eight items printed by the López de Haro firm up to 1700, eighty-nine of them by Tomás himself. Sixty-one of them have ten sheets or fewer, but some of those which have more are very large; indeed, hardly a year went by without the firm's managing to produce at least one substantial book. It began in 1678 with Juan Ronquillo's *Duelo espiritual*, two quarto volumes totalling just over ninety sheets, rose in 1683 to Gabriel de Aranda's life of the Cardinal Archbishop Agustín de Spínola (folio, 115 sheets), which was surpassed the following year by Gabriel de Santa María's *El predicador apostolico* (two folio volumes, 254 sheets in all). The firm printed five more books of more than 200 sheets before 1700, and Gabriel de Aranda beat his own record with the life of another religious, Fernando de Contreras, in 1692 (folio, 291 sheets). If religious biography in particular accounted for the largest items in terms of size, the topic of religion in general was by far the most important, with fifty-six of Tomás's items. News comes a poor second with twenty-three items, while medicine and popular literature are joint third with three each. Significantly, perhaps, the 'literature' includes a dramatic

[35] Aguilar Piñal, *Impresos sevillanos del siglo XVIII*, p. 13.

piece, *Alcazar de la razon, y centro de regocijo: zarzuela al parto de la Reina doña Maria de Orleans* (Escudero 1968, no date). The remaining items include history, law, a book on swordsmanship, and Luis de Valdivia's *Arte, y gramatica general de la lengua que corre en todo el Reyno de la Chile* of 1684.

There is evidence that Tomás published a news bulletin with the title *Diario*. This is probably to be translated not by English 'daily', but by the more elastic 'journal'. The Hispanic Society of America has ten issues for 1683, one of them numbered 26, and one issue for 1686 numbered 6; the British Library has number 3 for 1683 and number 5 for 1686; Montoto 210 records what appears to be number 2 for 1683. Our figures include only those preserved in these collections, not the inferential missing numbers.

Some of the minor 'printers' of this period are very shadowy figures. At least one was not a printer at all: we have seen an edition of the letters of St Jerome which bears the legend 'Apud Didacum Philippum de Urrieta', Seville 1670 (the copy in the library of Trinity College, Cambridge, III.8.168: see Escudero 1734). This book was manifestly not printed in Spain; it has an Antwerp *imprimatur* at the end, which suggests, together with its general appearance, that it was printed in the Spanish Netherlands for distribution in Spain. So Diego Felipe de Urrieta can have been no more than the publisher or seller of the book.

Thanks to Pepys, we have been able to examine an item ostensibly printed 'Por Pedro de Segura, Mercader de Libros, en la calle de Genova' with a licence dated 8 January 1670: an octavo edition of Ginés Pérez de Hita's *Historia de los vandos de los Zegries y Abencerrages* (Pepys 311, Gaselee 129). Escudero 1732 records the book, but he had never seen a copy. Segura's name appears to occur nowhere else, although he could conceivably have been a descendant of the original Bartolomé Segura of 1477. Of its nine typefaces, we have seen seven used by the widow Rodríguez in the period 1671–4, although one was on a different body; but López de Haro also used seven of the nine in the period 1679–84. If the date 1670 is genuine, Segura might have printed the book, only to die or retire and have his type bought by the widow Rodríguez; or the widow might have printed it for him, since they were neighbours in the Calle de Génova. If the date 1670 is false, the book must have been printed about ten years later by López de Haro, who had perhaps acquired some type formerly owned by the widow Rodríguez. We are inclined to think that the widow printed the book for Segura in 1670.

In 1673 one Pedro Castera printed a newsletter (B.L., 1323.g.1[15]). This is the only Seville item with his imprint, but the same name appears in Málaga in 1668 and in Saragossa in 1674. In 1676 Manuel Ramos printed another newsletter (B.L., 1445.f.17[61]); as pointed out earlier, the St John broadsides of 1674 do not clarify his status, but suggest that he was an employee, not his own master. Of more interest is Alonso Víctor de Paredes. Three flimsy items were printed under his name in Seville, dated 1674, 1675 and 1677. If this is not the Alonso de Paredes who printed in Madrid from about 1645 to 1651, he may be a son of the Madrid one, and perhaps a relative of the busy Madrid printer Julián de Paredes. (He may also have been related to the Francisco Carlos de Paredes whose name appears, along with that of Juan Francisco de Blas, on a St John broadside.) Alonso Víctor is remarkable for having written and printed a book on the art of printing. The book is now lost, since, somewhat eccentrically, he printed only one copy.[36] The career of Juan Antonio Tarazona is also a little puzzling: his name appears in Jerez imprints from 1671 to 1683 and in eleven Seville items ranging from 1682 to 1689 (or twelve items, if we count the appearance of his name on the St John broadside printed on the press of the widow Rodríguez in 1674). The puzzling thing is his apparent ability to run two

[36] See M. de Burgos, *Observaciones sobre el arte de la imprenta*, ed. A. Rodríguez-Moñino, Valencia, 1947, pp. 57–8. The book was written around 1680, when Paredes was about sixty-four; it still existed in the early nineteenth century.

presses, one in Jerez and the other in Seville, even for a short period. One item, a sermon by Francisco Pardo (1683 – Montoto 211) gives a tiny clue: it was printed 'en la Oficina de Juan Antonio Tarazona, impressor de libros, vive en la calle de Genova, en la casa del Beaterio'. This address in the Calle de Génova in 1683, and his connection with the widow Rodríguez – who lived there – in 1674, suggests that he acted as some sort of manager for the widow, while keeping on his own necessarily small business in Jerez, and that he eventually moved to Seville. He could then have worked for Cabezas, who inherited some of the widow's typographical material, until Cabezas stopped printing in 1681, which might have prompted his permanent move to Seville. All this is mere speculation, however; the only certainty is that he had his own stock of type, so that his work is typographically distinct from that of his contemporaries. Finally, there is one book printed in the College of San Buenaventura in 1687 (Escudero 1844). We suspect that this college, like that of San Hermenegildo, had a press on the premises which occasionally produced books for public circulation.

So far we have mentioned twenty-eight names which appear in some form in Seville imprints during the second half of the century. To get an idea of the number of firms which were active in this period, we must exclude about a dozen of these names: some because they were publishers, not printers; others because they were employees, not masters; and others like Pedro Castera or the religious houses, who produced so little that it would be misleading to include them. We have not dealt with Andrés Grande and Simón Faxardo, whose long careers extended from the first into the second half of the century, nor with Francisco Garay and Juan de la Puerta, who began to print late in the century. However, they bring the total back up to twenty. If we exclude the exceptional and unexplained case of Salvador de Cea Teza in 1654, the number of firms working in Seville during this half-century was never less than three or more than six (there were six from 1652 to

1654, but they include the shadowy figures Francisco Ignacio de Lyra and Juan Lorenzo Machado/Bispo). The corresponding range for Madrid during this period is nine-eighteen, precisely three times as many. On the other hand, Madrid had less than three times the total number of printers, which means that the average life-span of a printing firm was greater in Madrid than in Seville. This is not altogether surprising, since the turnover among Seville printers seems to have been rather greater. Gabriel Ramos Vejarano, Pedro Castera, Juan Vejarano and Juan Antonio Tarazona all moved to Seville from other, smaller Andalusian towns. If they profited by their move, they never became major printers. The typefounders Espinosa and Montoya, and the printers Bedmar, Juan de Ribera and Pedro Castera left Seville and went to Mexico, Madrid or Saragossa. Mexico was an expanding market, Madrid offered the best hope of security in Castile, while Saragossa, capital of Aragon, avoided the worst effects of the slump which overtook the book trade in Castile. Castera, who, perhaps significantly, had already moved once, was the only one of this group not to succeed. (Bedmar, it may be remembered, turned down an invitation to go back to Andalusia.)

Alonso Víctor de Paredes (assuming that there was only one person of this name), who was born in Madrid in 1616, was the only printer of this period to move from the capital to Seville. His length of stay there is in doubt, but he was back in Madrid when he came to write his book; neither move seems to have brought him much success. The numbers involved in these migrations are small and therefore statistically invalid, but they give the impression that there was more to be gained by moving from Seville than to it.

Seven of the firms we have examined in detail printed more than twenty items which have been recorded: J. F. de Blas (?1667–1700+), N. Rodríguez and his widow (1638–74), J. de Ossuna (1652–?81), T. de D. Miranda (1666–78), J. Cabezas (?1675–81), J. Vejarano (1681–3) and T. López de Haro and his heirs (1678–1700+). In all, they produced in the seventeenth century a total of 379 signed or readily attributable items, an average of only 2·7 per year each. A total of 267, or seventy per cent, had ten sheets or fewer. If we add to these totals the thirty-two pieces of imprintless ephemera which in the course of this study we attribute to these printers, the average output rises slightly to 2·9, the percentage of ephemera to nearly 73. The percentage of truly ephemeral material is probably lower, since material of this sort is not defined by number of sheets but by binding, or rather lack of binding. Single sheets were generally sold folded. Ephemeral items of more than one sheet were sold stabbed; we have seen examples which were given wrappers before being stabbed, the wrapper sometimes having a manuscript title. Few such pamphlets have survived as issued, so it is hard to know where the line was drawn: to some degree it depended on format. For example, a 16° regularly had fewer than ten sheets, but unless it was very slim, it had to be bound rather than stabbed, since the two extra folds made it much thicker than a quarto with the same number of sheets. On the other hand, the notoriously low survival rate of true ephemera means that this class of printed matter is greatly under-represented in the collections of today.

As for subject-matter, religion easily comes first, with almost half (forty-eight per cent); if this figure were expressed in printed sheets, it would be even higher, since most large books fall into the category. News comes second, with exactly a quarter (twenty-five per cent), and literature (mostly 'popular') third with sixteen per cent. Medicine comes a poor fourth with well under three per cent. To some extent we can guess why the printers' output is made up in this way. Seville was an old cathedral city, the home of many different religious organisations, and many of the larger religious works were undoubtedly commissioned. The same can probably be said of the much smaller number of medical works. Most of the small religious items and virtually all the news and literature were produced to meet public demand, as is clear from the format, usually single sheets folded as quarto. News items, by their nature, were often original editions, especially if the source of the news was the Mediterranean or the Indies. News from northern Europe, on the other hand, was often reprinted from Madrid newsletters. Literature was almost entirely reprinted.

From the viewpoint of culture and the advancement of human knowledge, Seville in the second half of the seventeenth century is therefore extremely depressing. Good literature was no longer being written there, and much of what was being printed was bad. The standard and content of news was inferior to that of the poorest modern newspapers. The works emanating from the university's once reputable medical faculty included arid squabbles about the folly or wisdom of drawing blood from patients' ankles; and while the large corpus of religious material may contain many examples of true piety, we look in vain for dynamic theology. True, contemporary Madrid was little better, especially after the death of Calderón in 1681. It may be significant that Seville's only major original contributions were in fields where Madrid could not easily compete: trade and navigation. Apart from this, Seville strikes us as being very provincial in the most pejorative sense of the word. As we shall see presently, this word may also fairly be applied to the booksellers whom Pepys must have visited. We say 'must', because he bought enough large items to give the lie to one of the notes scribbled in his journal during his stay in Spain: 'no books, only sold by the blind'.[37] The reference is to the ephemeral matter of which Pepys 1545 and 1553 are composed, and which was sold in the streets by blind pedlars; if it is an exaggeration, it is a pardonable one. It is also a sorry epitaph for what had once been the centre of the Castilian book trade.

[37] W. Matthews, 'Samuel Pepys and Spain', p. 128.

CHAPTER THREE

The Printers of Pepys 1553 and their Type

THE study of the output of Seville printers will not help us much to identify those who printed the plays bought by Pepys: none of them is remarkable for his record of play-printing. Even if any of them were, this would scarcely be conclusive. We shall therefore rely on typographical evidence. Our manner of procedure was to list all the typefaces and typographical ornaments used in the *sueltas*, noting wear, damage, adulteration and, where relevant, body-size. This list is reproduced below. We then noted the Seville printers who used this material in the period 1650–84 (especially 1670–84), and the dates when they did so. An abbreviated version of these findings is added to the list. We next made a table for each *suelta*, listing in it each typeface or ornament used in the *suelta*, together with the names of the printers known to have used them, and the date of use. In most cases one name in particular recurred at a series of appropriate dates, giving a clear indication of the printer of the *suelta* and an approximate date. We do not reproduce these lengthy individual tables, but interested readers will find it possible to reconstruct them from the information supplied. We have illustrated all the types and ornaments used in the *sueltas*, identifying them where possible by name of cutter, and by early specimens in which they appeared. Where this was not possible we try to mention some book or other (not always Spanish) in which we have seen them, but we must emphasise that this part of our work was by no means systematic.

ROMAN TYPES

R1: 1, 21, 24. :16.5 mm titling capitals, as shown in the specimen of the widow Elsevier (Amsterdam, 1681). The types illustrated in the specimen are attributed to Christoffel van Dyck, but there is no evidence that he cut this face.[1] We have seen it as early as the *Obras de don Luis de Gongora*, Brussels, F. Foppens, 1659. Slight damage to the letters MED of 1 is also visible in 24. Used by the widow Rodríguez 1671–4, J. F. de Blas 1672–7, Miranda 1675, Paredes 1675, Cabezas 1676–8, Ramos 1676.

R2: 7. :16 mm titling capitals, unidentified, but originating in the Low Countries, *c.* 1550–1600.[2] Used by Cabezas 1674, López de Haro 1683.

R3: 4, 12, 17, 20, 21. The :13 mm titling capitals of the 1628 Vatican specimen, first definite use in Rome 1614, common in Spain from 1621 (though they appear on a title-page with the dubious date 1614).[3] Damaged M in 4 recurs in 17; damaged D in 17 recurs in 20. Used by J. F. de Blas 1668–77, widow Rodríguez 1671, Miranda 1675–8, Ramos 1676, heirs of J. G. de Blas 1678.

R4: 5, 27, 28. Unidentified :11.5 mm titling capitals, perhaps a copy of Van den Keere's *capitales de trois règles médiane*

[1] See John Dreyfus (ed.), *Type specimen facsimiles* [hereafter *TSF*], London, 1963–72, i, no. 12 (also 13, 15). The material in this specimen was no doubt available from the foundry of Van Dyck (*c.* 1606–69/70), but there is no evidence that he cut this face. The M and E actually appear first on the specimen of B. Voskens, Hamburg, 1660 (*TSF*, i, no. 6).

[2] We thank Mr Nicolas Barker for this information.

[3] See *The type specimen of the Vatican Press 1628*, ed. H. D. L. Vervliet, Amsterdam, 1967, item 27. For the dubious 1614 title-page, see below, p. 104, n. 26; even if our guess-date is wrong, it would be unwise to take this suspicious date at face value.

(which are :11 mm).[4] Seen as early as Fernando de Herrera, *Versos* (Seville, G. Ramos Vejarano, 1619), also in M. Bonacina, *Opera omnia* (Antwerp, J. Meursius, 1632), and in other Flemish books. Flemish? Used by J. G. de Blas 1642–58, Cabezas 1675–8, Vejarano 1682, J. F. de Blas 1682 (in 28, which bears his imprint).

R5: 18. :11 mm capitals, illustrated as *parysse canon romein* in the specimen of J. Enschedé, Haarlem, 1768.[5] Used by J. F. de Blas 1673 (doubtful), widow Rodríguez 1673–4, Cabezas 1674–81, López de Haro 1679–83.

R6: 8, 14. Unidentified :9 mm capitals. Worn, with damage to M in both, also adulterated in both with E and O from R9. Used by J. F. de Blas 1673–6 with the same adulteration.

R7: 27, 28. Unidentified :9 mm capitals, seen in the *Obras* of Baltasar Gracián (Antwerp, J. and J. B. Verdussen, 1669). Mixed with R8 in 27. Used by Cabezas 1676–9, J. F. de Blas 1682 (in 28).

R8: 1, 5, 11, 13, 19, 22, 24, 27. The :8.3 mm *dubbelde augustijn* capitals of the widow Elsevier's specimen of Amsterdam, 1681.[6] A damaged M recurs in 13, 19 and 22. Mixed with R7 in 27. Used by widow Rodríguez 1674, Cabezas 1676–80, Vejarano 1681–2.

R9: 2, 4, 6, 8, 10, 12, 14, 15, 16, 17, 20, 21, 23, 25, 26. The :8.2 mm capitals attributed to Peter Schoeffer the Younger.[7] Common in Spain. A foreign A in 2 appears to recur in 15 and 25. A different foreign A in 6 recurs in 23. Only E and O are present in 8 and 14, mixed with R6. Only F, A, A are present in 16, mixed with R10. A dam-

[4] For Van den Keere's typeface, see Vervliet, *Sixteenth-century printing types of the Low Countries*, Amsterdam, 1968, pp. 224–5.

[5] See the *Proef van letteren welke gegooten worden in de Nieuwe Haerlemsche Lettergietery van J. Enschedé*, Haarlem, 1768 (information from Mr N. Barker).

[6] *TSF*, i, 12 (also 11 and 15). Like R1, available from Van Dyck's foundry, but with no evidence that he cut it.

[7] See Vervliet, *Sixteenth-century printing types . . .*, pp. 238–9.

aged A recurs in 17 and 20. Used by widow Rodríguez 1671, Ossuna 1671–81, J. F. de Blas 1673–6 (adulterated with R6), Miranda (adulterated as 2, 1675; as 6, 1678), Cabezas 1678, Vejarano 1682.

R10: 8, 10, 14, 16. Granjon's *capitales sur deux lignes de cicéro* (:7 mm).[8] Common in Spain. Mixed with R9 in 16, used at the end (FIN) in the others. Used by widow Rodríguez 1671, Miranda 1671, J. F. de Blas 1669–76.

R11: 27. :6.8 mm capitals shown as the *kleine canon romein no. 4* in the Ploos van Amstel specimen of 1784.[9] Used by Cabezas 1675–81, Vejarano 1682–3.

R12: 3, 7, 18. Unidentified :6.2 mm capitals. Worn, perhaps impure. Used by widow Rodríguez 1671–3 (different T), Cabezas 1676–9 (doubtful), López de Haro 1679–83 (as in the three *sueltas*).

R13: 9. The capitals (:6 mm) of the *petit canon romain* of Granjon.[10] Used by Miranda 1671, heirs of J. G. de Blas 1678.

R14: 1, 5, 11, 13, 19, 22, 27. An *ascendonica* roman available from the foundry of Dirck Voskens, and shown on his widow's specimens of Amsterdam, *c.* 1695.[11] Capitals occasionally used in F. Strada, *Guerras de Flandes*, vol. i (Cologne, 1682) (e.g. p. 38). The lower case is present in *suelta* 5, where, if the two lines are set solid, the body-size can be calculated at a little more than 160 mm/20 lines. The capitals are used in 5 and 11 with the capitals of R21 as small caps. Used by widow Rodríguez 1671–4, Cabezas 1675–81, Vejarano 1681–3. The cap/small cap

[8] Displayed in Plantin's *Index characterum* of 1567, and used by him from that date; see *TSF*, ii, p. 2, no. 2.

[9] See the *Proef van romeinsche, cursyfsche . . . en anderen letteren . . . welke gegooten worden by geb. Ploos van Amstel . . .*, Amsterdam, [1784] (information from Mr N. Barker).

[10] The capitals first appeared in 1547. See *TSF*, ii, p. 3, no. 17.

[11] *TSF*, i, 8 (lines 3 and 4) and 9 (line 3). This face is different in design and in body-size from the *ascendonica romein* displayed on *TSF*, i, 9. There is no proof that Voskens was the cutter.

mixture of R14 and R21 was used by widow Rodríguez 1671–4, Cabezas 1679–81.

R15: 3, 18. Unidentified :5 mm capitals. Seen in Strada, *Guerras de Flandes*, i (Cologne, 1682), translator's preface. Used by widow Rodríguez 1673–4, López de Haro 1679–84.

R16: 28. Unidentified :4.7 mm capitals. Used by J. F. de Blas 1682 (in 28), López de Haro 1683.

R17: 9, 13, 16, 19, 27. Granjon's *parangon romain*.[12] Common throughout Spain. Foreign J and/or U in 19 and 27 (lacking in Granjon's original). Used by widow Rodríguez 1671, J. F. de Blas 1669–76, Cabezas 1674–80 (with foreign J/U from 1676), Ramos 1676, Ossuna 1681, Vejarano 1681–3 (with foreign J/U).

R18: 4, 6, 15, 17, 20, 21, 22, 23, 26. Garamont's *parangonne romaine*.[13] Common throughout Spain. Used for running-heads in 20, 21, 23 and 26, worn in all nine *sueltas*. Capitals used by Miranda 1675–8, with lower case in Pepys 1545(17), which has his imprint but no date; also worn.

R19: 1, 4, 6, 10, 12, 15, 17, 19, 20, 21, 22, 23, 24, 25, 26, 27. The *texte romain* attributed to Garamont.[14] Common throughout Spain. Foreign sorts in 4, 6, 12, 15, 17, 20, 21, 23, 25. Measurable in 4, 25 and 27 as approximately 116 mm/20 lines, otherwise leaded or in single lines. Used by Miranda 1675–8 (foreign sorts as 4, 6, 12, etc.), Cabezas 1675–81, J. F. de Blas 1676–7, heirs of J. G. de Blas 1678, Ossuna 1680–1, Vejarano 1682–3.

R20: 3, 7, 18, 27. A text-type shown in Loyson's *Epreuve des caractères d'imprimerie venant d'Hollande*, Paris, 1728.[15] Seen in Gerónimo de Cancer, *Obras varias* (Lisbon,

[12] *TSF*, i, 4 and 15. Plantin had a set of matrices by 1588.

[13] *TSF*, ii, p. 3, no. 20.

[14] *TSF*, ii, p. 3, no. 22.

[15] See Marius Audin, *Les livrets typographiques des fonderies françaises créées avant 1800*, Amsterdam, 1964, plate XXII, p. 65.

1657), Strada, *Guerras de Flandes*, i (Cologne, 1682) and in English books of this period. Dutch? Measurable as 116 mm/20 lines in 27, where it is also rather worn. Used by widow Rodríguez 1671–4, Cabezas 1675–8 (worn), López de Haro 1679–83.

R21: 5, 11. Unidentified :3.4 mm roman capitals, used as small caps with R14. Used in the same way by widow Rodríguez 1671–4, Cabezas 1679–81.

R22: 13, 28. A corrupted version of Sanlecque's copy of Garamont's *St Augustin* (see R23); it may be compared with the *Saint Augustin a son oeil romain* shown by Delacolonge and the *No 7 Augustyn Romein* of Ploos van Amstel.[16] In 28, the body is 94.5 mm/20 lines, in 13 there is only one line (Hablan en ella . . .). Used by Cabezas 1679–81, Vejarano 1681–3, J. F. de Blas 1682 (in 28).

R23: 8, 14, 27. Garamont's *St Augustin*.[17] Capitals only in 27. Adapted in 8 and 14 to produce a smaller body (86 mm/20 lines) by using caps and x-height lower case letters from the original, ascenders and descenders probably made up in Spain. Original version used by Cabezas 1674–7; for adaptation, see R26.

R24: 3. Unidentified roman capitals, *c.* :3.3 mm. Used by López de Haro 1679–83.

R25: 9. Unidentified roman capitals, *c.* :3.3 mm. No user recorded.

R26: 8, 14. The adapted Garamont *St Augustin* described under R23. Although we list it under R23, for the purposes of evidence it must be treated as a different face, hence this entry. Several adaptations of Garamont's *St Augustin* seem to have been made in Spain in the second half of the seventeenth century; this one is notable for its 'compressed' and ugly g, and because j, p and q are cast

[16] See *The type specimen of Delacolonge*, ed. Harry Carter, Amsterdam, 1969, pp. 31, 85 and 116, and the notes, p. 52; for Ploos van Amstel, see note 9 above.

[17] *TSF*, ii, p. 4, no. 24.

high on their bodies. In Seville only J. F. de Blas (1673) had this adaptation, but it was used at the same time in Madrid, where it was probably cast.

R27: Unidentified roman text-type, 86 mm/20 lines, cast from badly justified matrices. The bad casting may be connected with adaptation to reduce body-size, as with R26: b, d, ſt, ſſ and f seem foreign, too small for the rest; p and q are cast high, ſ and l low on the body. No user recorded for this body-size, but see R27B.

R27B: 4, 15, 17, 23. Face R27 (or most of it), cast on a body of 83 mm/20 lines, but with a wider set. There is a different (and larger) d, and while l is still cast low, other letters are better aligned. Used in this state, and on this body, by Miranda 1678.

R28: 16. Granjon's *gros cicéro romain*, here 85 mm/20 lines.[18] Some js are foreign, with two dots. This face, with the odd j, was very common in Madrid 1664–76, and this fount was almost certainly cast there. We have seen only J. F. de Blas use it in Seville (1672) on this body, but without the j. Miranda had a fount of R30 in 1671 which apparently had a few R28 sorts in it, including a two-dot j, but we measured the body as 86 mm.

R29: 7, 18. Roman text-type, here 86 mm/20 lines, with a very narrow set. An impure version of an original almost certainly cut by Haultin; it most closely resembles the *cicero antiqua* of J. P. Fievet's specimen of Frankfurt, 1664, which is an impure version of Haultin's *cicéro romain* as shown by J. A. Schmidt, *c.* 1695.[19] No user recorded.

[18] First used about 1568 (and in Seville by Hernando Díaz as early as 1571; we have noted it ourselves in his Juan Manuel, *El conde Lucanor*, 1575); ascender and descender sorts were shown in Plantin's folio specimen (see *TSF*, ii, p. 9, no. 37), the whole face in the Fuhrmann specimen (Nuremberg, 1616). It is also shown in the specimens of Frankfurt, 1664, and Amsterdam, 1681 (*TSF*, i, 4, 12 and 13).

[19] *TSF*, i, 4 (Fievet); see also i, 14 (393) and 15 for Haultin's *cicéro romain*.

R30: 9. A roman text-type (86 mm/20 lines in this *suelta*) used by Berton, his widow and his successor Jean Portau in La Rochelle, 1563–89.[20] Common in the Madrid area from 1619, this fount probably cast there. Used by Miranda 1671 on this body, but with some sorts (including two-dot j) from R28.

R31: 10. Unidentified roman text-type, *c.* 84 mm/20 lines, very worn. Some sorts like their counterparts in Lamesle's *Cicero romain oeil moyen, numero XXX*.[21] No user recorded.

R32: 5, 13, 19, 27, 28. Garamont's (?) *cicéro romain*.[22] 84 mm/20 lines in 5, 13, 19 and 27, unmeasurable in 28, which may be a different fount. Used by Cabezas 1675–81, Vejarano 1682 (apparently 85 mm/20 lines), J. F. de Blas 1682 (in 28).

R33: 11. Possibly the same face as R32, but cast on a smaller body (81.5 mm), and with a narrower set. This version used by widow Rodríguez 1671–4.

R34: 2, 12, 20, 21, 25, 26. Unidentified, adulterated text-type (79.5 mm). Some descenders cast high, ascenders cast low on the body, as in R27; it has some letters in common with Lamesle's *Cicero romain gros oeil moyen, numero XXXIII*.[23] The M is of ancient design, with double serifs on the tops of the legs. Worn in all six *sueltas*. Capitals (including M) used by Miranda 1675; the whole fount was used to print two other *sueltas*, neither with date or imprint, but both decorated with one of Miranda's woodblocks (see p. 56 below, and illustration).

R35: 1. Unidentified :2.7 mm capitals used as small caps in the act-heading. Used by Cabezas in Pepys 1545/24/8 and

[20] See L. Desgraves, *L'imprimerie à La Rochelle*, Geneva, 1960, 3 vols.

[21] See *The type-specimens of Claude Lamesle*, introd. by A. F. Johnson, Amsterdam, 1965. The amount of wear is too great for identification of the individual sorts to be certain.

[22] Cf. *TSF*, ii, p. 4, no. 26.

[23] For the Lamesle specimen, see note 21.

34/35 (undated) as small caps with R19.

R36: 3. Unidentified roman text-type (69 mm/20 lines), with some resemblances to the *descendiaen* of the widow Voskens's specimens of Amsterdam, *c.* 1695.[24] Used by López de Haro 1683–4, same body and condition.

R37: 11. Small roman capitals, unidentified, but similar in design to R20, with which they are used as small caps. Used in the same way by the widow Rodríguez 1673.

R38: 1, 13, 28. Granjon's *Granjonne*, used for text in 1, where it is 68.5 mm/20 lines.[25] Used by Cabezas 1675–6, Vejarano 1682–3, J. F. de Blas 1682 (in 28).

R39: 22, 24. Worn, unidentified roman text-type, 67.5 mm/20 lines. Some features reminiscent of Haultin?[26] Used by widow Rodríguez 1673–4, Cabezas 1678.

R40: 19. Apparently the capitals of Granjon's *Gaillarde*, used as small caps in the act-heading.[27] No user recorded.

R41: 28. Very small roman capitals, unidentified. Used by Vejarano 1683, and in this item (J. F. de Blas 1682).

[24] *TSF*, i, 8 and 9.

[25] *TSF*, i, 4, 9, 10 and 14. Plantin bought a strike in 1569.

[26] Mr N. Barker suggests to us that this face is reminiscent of Haultin's style, and that it may be an earlier version of the face shown as Lamesle XIX and Delacolonge p. 20 (*petit romain gros oeil*) (see notes 16 and 21 above).

[27] *TSF*, ii, p. 10, nos. 56 and 67. A specimen dated 1570 survives (*TSF*, ii, p. 14, no. 21).

ITALIC TYPES

IT1: 1, 19, 28. Granjon's *ascendonica cursive*.[28] Supposedly used only in the Plantin-Moretus house, although we have seen it in the Verdussens' printing of the *Obras* of Gracián (Antwerp, 1669). Also seen in Seville from 1633, and used by Cabezas 1675–81, Vejarano 1682, J. F. de Blas 1683 (as well as in 28, 1682).

IT2: 5, 9, 13, 24. Granjon's *parangon cursive*.[29] Common throughout Spain. Very worn in 9, less so in the rest; five lines in 9 are 33 mm, equal to 132 mm/20 lines. Used by J. F. de Blas 1672–6, Cabezas 1674–80, heirs of J. G. de Blas 1678, Vejarano 1683. The widow Rodríguez leaded out a smaller Granjon italic for this body in 1671, which suggests that she lacked this face.

IT3: 5, 19, 22, 27. The *italique de gros romain* of Jean Jannon, as shown in his specimen of Sedan, 1621.[30] Seen in Miguel de Barrios, *Las poesias famosas, y comedias* (Antwerp, the Verdussens, 1674). Two lines in 5 measure approximately 11.5 mm, i.e. about 116 mm/20 (cf. the body-size of R19 and R20). Mixed with IT4 in 5, 19 and 27. Used by Cabezas 1675–81 (with IT4 mixed in 1676–9), Vejarano 1681–3.

IT4: 2, 5, 19, 27. Guyot's *texte italique*.[31] Common in Spain. Pure but worn in 2, a few sorts mixed with IT3 in the

[28] *TSF*, ii, p. 8, no. 10; cut in 1570. We have also seen Adrien Hubert of Antwerp use it in *Theatre des cruautez des hereticques de nostre temps*, 1588. For IT1, IT2, IT6, IT7, IT10, IT11 and IT13, see also A. F. Johnson, 'The italic types of Robert Granjon', *The Library*, IV, xxi (1940–1), 291–7; we use his nomenclature for the 'second' and 'third' *St Augustins* of Granjon.

[29] *TSF*, ii, p. 3, no. 21.

[30] See *The type specimen of Jean Jannon*, ed. Paul Beaujon, Paris, 1927.

[31] Vervliet, *Sixteenth-century printing types . . .*, pp. 288–9.

others. Used pure by widow Rodríguez 1671–4, Miranda 1675, J. F. de Blas 1676, Cabezas 1677, López de Haro 1678–83. Used mixed by Cabezas 1676–9 (with IT3).

IT5: 10. The letters *CA* of this may be Granjon's 'third' *texte italique*.[32] The other letters are not, and we have not identified them. We have seen the Granjon used by some Seville printers, but we have not seen this particular mixture in any signed work.

IT6: 1, 11, 19, 22, 24, 28. Granjon's 'third' *St Augustin cursif*, the equivalent of 94 mm/20 lines in 1.[33] Common in Seville, with the original small *M* (as here), rarer elsewhere (Madrid printers used a larger foreign *M*). Used by widow Rodríguez 1672–4, Cabezas 1675–81, Miranda 1678 (lower case only, with capitals from a Granjon *texte italique*), Vejarano 1681–3, J. F. de Blas (in 28, 1682), López de Haro 1683–4. Cabezas had a version with foreign *M* and *v*, date uncertain, but there is no sign of it in the *sueltas*.

IT7: 8, 14. Granjon's 'second' *St Augustin cursif*,[34] here adapted to an 86 mm body by the use of some foreign (and smaller) descenders, such as *g* and *q*, and by casting *p* high on the body. This adaptation was common in the Madrid area from about 1650, but we have seen it in Seville only in J. F. de Blas 1673.

IT8: 3, 18. A medium-sized italic, in running-heads. Used by López de Haro 1683.

IT9: 9. Italic text-type common in Madrid area from 1619; here 86 mm/20 lines. A copy of IT6, perhaps related to another copy, the *corsivo silvio* of the Vatican foundry.[35] This version used by Miranda 1671.

[32] For the true Granjon, see *TSF*, ii, p. 4, no. 23; also *TSF*, i, 2 and 3.

[33] *TSF*, ii, p. 9, no. 27.

[34] Johnson, 'The italic types of Robert Granjon', fig. 2, type no. 3.

[35] See note 33 and *The type specimen of the Vatican Press 1628*, no. 40.

IT10: 7, 18. Granjon's *médiane cursive droite*, here 86 mm/20 lines.[36] No user of this body-size recorded, but see IT10B and C.

IT10B: 5, 13, 19, 22, 27. The same face as IT10, measurable as 84 mm/20 lines in all but 27, which is included tentatively on other evidence. Used on this body by Cabezas 1676–81.

IT10C: 11. The same face as IT10, 81.5 mm/20 lines. Used on this body by widow Rodríguez 1674.

IT11: 16. Granjon's *médiane cursive pendante*, here 85mm/20 lines.[37] Rare in Spain. Used only by López de Haro 1683 on this body.

IT12: 10. Haultin's '*médiane italique maigre*' (?), here 84 mm/20 lines. This typeface appears in none of the specimens that we have seen and, to our knowledge, has not been attributed to Haultin in any published work.[38] However, we have seen it used in England in 1553–7, in Florence and in Venice in 1574, in Alcalá in 1588, and also in Valencia, Barcelona and Antwerp (though not in Seville).[39] This distribution is entirely consistent with Haultin's having cut the face, for various types of his were exported to England and Italy during his lifetime. There are also distinct resemblances between this design and that of smaller italics attributed to him.[40] We adopt the name *médiane italique maigre* by analogy

[36] *TSF*, ii, p. 4, no. 28.

[37] *TSF*, ii, p. 4, no. 27; and p. 9, no. 39.

[38] The main study of the Haultin press (Desgraves, *L'imprimerie à La Rochelle*, ii, *Les Haultin*) does not help.

[39] For England, see F. S. Isaac, *English printers' types of the sixteenth century*, Oxford, 1963, plates 40a, 59, 62b; for Florence, see S. Morison, *Four centuries of fine printing*, London, 1960, p. 88; and for Venice, see L. Dolce, *Le vite di tutti gl'imperatori romani*, Venice, Bonelli, 1574. Dr Vervliet tells us that the typeface 'occurs frequently in Parisian printing from 1550 on'.

[40] E.g. the *gaillarde italique* on p. 16 of the Delacolonge specimen, which Carter attributes to Haultin; or his *nompareille cursive* of *TSF*, ii, p. 5, no. 39.

with the *médiane italique grasse* which has been attributed to him.[41]

IT13: 6. Granjon *cicéro cursive*, no. 4 in Johnson, here 86 mm/20 lines.[42] The flamboyant original *v* has been replaced, as it often was, by a more sober one (apparently from Granjon's *médiane cursive pendante*, IT11), cast too low on the body. No user recorded, but see below, IT13C.

IT13B: 4, 15, 17, 23. The face of IT13 on an 83 mm body. The same foreign *v* is present, but cast too high. No user recorded for this body.

IT13C: 2, 12, 20, 21, 25, 26. The face of IT13 on a 79.5 mm body. The same foreign *v*, also a foreign *z* with a tail like Tavernier's.[43] This face, on this body, was used in two imprintless *sueltas* decorated with one of Miranda's blocks (see R34 above).

IT14: 3. A small italic possibly cut by Tavernier, called 'de Laet's' by Vervliet after its first user.[44] Here 69 mm/20 lines, with foreign *g* and *v*, but still showing the striking original *z*. Rare anywhere, in Spain only in López de Haro 1684, same body, same adulteration.

IT15: 1. Apparently Granjon's *Valentine*, here 68.5 mm/20 lines.[45] Used by Cabezas 1675, Vejarano 1682–3, López de Haro 1683.

IT16: 1, 22, 24. Unidentified text italic, 67.5 mm/20 lines. Some capitals (notably *M* and *R*) from Tavernier's *philosophie italique*.[46] Used by widow Rodríguez 1674, Cabezas 1678. Only a few Tavernier capitals are present in 1, mixed with IT15.

[41] See A. Tinto, 'I tipi della Stamperia del Popolo Romano (1561–1570)', *Gutenberg-Jahrbuch* 1967, 26–38, illustration p. 35; and *Il corsivo nella tipografia del Cinquecento*, Milan, 1972, pp. 84–7 and illustration xxix.

[42] Johnson, 'The italic types of Robert Granjon', fig. 3.

[43] For Tavernier's *z* on this body, see Vervliet, *Sixteenth-century printing types . . .*, pp. 298–9.

[44] Vervliet, *Sixteenth-century printing types . . .*, pp. 302–3.

[45] *TSF*, ii, p. 10, no. 54.

[46] Vervliet, *Sixteenth-century printing types . . .*, pp. 304–5. The Tavernier face is also shown in the Fievet specimen of Frankfurt, 1682 (*TSF*, i, 5).

METAL ORNAMENTS*

M1: 2, 4, 15, 23. 'Ropework', *c.* 10 by 3 mm per unit, in a line across the page. Copy of a Parisian design of *c.* 1510.[47] Used by Cabezas 1676–80, Miranda 1678.

M2: 5. Shown as item N in the *vignettes au corps de gros romain* of Lamesle's specimen of Paris, 1742, origin unknown.[48] Used by Cabezas 1675–7, Vejarano 1682–3.

M3: 5, 28. Eight-pointed stars, diameter *c.* 3.4 mm. Used by Cabezas 1679, J. F. de Blas 1682 (in 28).

M4: 6. The pagoda-like *vignettes de parangon* of Granjon, first used 1562, by Granjon himself in 1584, and illustrated in the fifth row of the flowers in the specimen of the widow Adamszoon and A. Ente, Amsterdam, *c.* 1700.[49] Used by Miranda 1678, Cabezas 1681, both worn.

M5: 6, 12, 20, 21, 26. Shown as item R in the *vignettes au corps de petit romain* of Lamesle's specimen (Paris, 1742), origin unknown.[50] Used in a line across the page, below the *reparto*, with the addition of pieces of M7 and M8 at the ends of the line in 12, 20, 21, 26. Used by Miranda, no date.[51]

* Excluding rules.

47 It may be seen in the *Quincuplex Psalterium* of Paris, H. Estienne, 1513.
48 For Lamesle specimen, see note 21.
49 *TSF*, i, 11; shown also by Lamesle (see note 21) as *vignettes de petit parangon*, item B, and Delacolonge, *vignettes*, no. 236, p. 68 of the facsimile. For the attribution to Granjon, see pp. 65–6 of the introduction to the Delacolonge facsimile.
50 See note 21.
51 See Santiago Montoto, *Impresos sevillanos*, Madrid, 1948, no. 234, and the plate facing p. 92, where it is shown as a title-page border.

M6: 8, 14. Fleurs-de-lys, 8 by 9 mm, as tailpieces in both. No user recorded.

M7: 4, 12, 15, 20, 21, 26. Fist, seen from the back, showing four fingers and an ornate cuff (7 by 4 mm). Combined with M5 and M8 in 12, 20, 21 and 26. Used by Miranda 1675, Cabezas 1679.

M8: 12, 20, 21, 26. Maltese cross 4 mm square. Combined with M5 and M7 in all four. No user recorded. Adulterated with a foreign cross in 12 and 21.

M9: 13. The fists shown on Konrad Berner's Frankfurt specimen of 1592.[52] Used by Cabezas 1680, Vejarano 1682.

M10: 14. One of the parts of the Granjon fleuron on the title-page of Plantin's *Index characterum* of 1567.[53] Very worn. No user recorded.

M11: 16. Hollow-centred asterisks, as shown on the specimen of J. P. Fievet, Frankfurt, 1664; origin unknown.[54] As tailpieces. Used for the same purpose by J. G. de Blas 1639.

M12: 19, 22, 24. Fists, seen from the back, with small cuff and protruding thumb. Used in pairs, end-to-end, in the line with the words JORNADA PRIMERA in all three. 4.8 by 3 mm. Used by Cabezas 1679.

M13: 27. An arabesque fleuron attributable to Granjon, and shown on the 1592 Berner specimen.[55] Used by widow Rodríguez 1673, Cabezas 1675–6, Vejarano 1683.

M14: 27. Part of the Granjon fleuron on the title-page of Plantin's *Index characterum* of 1567; Plantin had bought

[52] *TSF*, i, 2: the forefinger of the fist (one of three on the sheet) points to Granjon's *médiane italique droite*.

[53] *TSF*, ii, p. 5, no. 46. Also shown in the outer border of the Berner specimens of 1592 and 1622 (*TSF*, i, 2 and 3) and separately by Delacolonge as *vignette* no. 212.

[54] *TSF*, i, 4: see the *cicero*.

[55] *TSF*, i, 2. Also shown by Delacolonge, p. 68; for the attribution to Granjon, see the Delacolonge introduction, p. 65.

the matrices from Granjon the previous year.[56] Used by Vejarano, no date, but 1681–3, and in 1683.

M15: 28. Item U in the *suite des vignettes de cicero* of Lamesle's Paris specimen of 1742, origin unknown.[57] Cast from a badly-justified matrix such that the right-hand side prints only when there is no other type to the right of it. Used by Cabezas 1676, Vejarano 1682, J. F. de Blas 1682 (in 28).

M16: 28. The large acorns, 4 by 6.8 mm, of the 1592 Berner specimen (see under 'Cursiff Parangon de GranIon').[58] Used by Vejarano 1682, J. F. de Blas 1682 (in 28).

M17: 2. Leaves, 5 by 3.3 mm, as tailpieces. No user recorded. Illustrated as item H in the *Vignettes au corps de Petit Romain* of the 1742 Lamesle specimen.[59]

[56] *TSF*, ii, p. 5, no. 46; see also *TSF*, ii, p. 14, no. 21. Also illustrated by Lamesle, *Suite des Vignettes de gros romain*, item LO.

[57] See note 21.

[58] *TSF*, i, 2. See also Lamesle, *Vignettes au Corps de Cicero*, item N.

[59] Also Delacolonge, *vignette* no. 103 (see introduction, p. 62). A smaller version of the same design appears on the 1592 Berner sheet (*TSF*, i, 2).

WOODBLOCKS

W1: 4, 21. Vase of flowers, 65 by 60 mm. Used by Miranda 1675.

W2: 5, 22, 27. Swag, 105 by 77 mm. Used by Cabezas 1676, Vejarano 1682.

W3: 18. Vase of flowers, 51 by 54 mm. No user recorded.

W4: 24. Basket of flowers, 85 by 64 mm. Used by Cabezas 1676 and 1679, Vejarano no date (but 1681–3).

W5: 27. Initial A, 12.5 by 12 mm. Matches a set used by Cabezas 1676.

W6: 27. Initial N, 12.5mm square. Part of the same set as W5.

W7: 27. Initial E, 12.5 mm square. Part of the same set as W5.

W8: 28. Vase of flowers, 73 by 63 mm. Used by J. F. de Blas 1676, 1682 (in 28).

W9: 28. Initial D, 34 by 36mm. In this item only, J. F. de Blas 1682.

W10: 28. Initial E with bird, 35 by 33 mm. In this item only, J. F. de Blas 1682.

W11: A large woodblock not found in Pepys 1553 at all, but used twice in items with Miranda's imprint: *Curioso romance que manifiesta, los celebres regocijos, que . . . se consagraron, al . . . nuebo govierno, de . . . D. Carlos II* (1675), and *Milicia angelica de Santo Tomas de Aquino* (1678), to be found in B.L. 811.e.51, items 15 and 32. The same block (85 by 98 mm) is present in *sueltas* of *El imposible mas facil* (B.L., T.1737[12]) and *A vn tiempo rey y vassallo* (B.L., 11725.b.6[10]).[60] In all four cases it is used as a tailpiece. The text type of the two *sueltas* is

[60] The first is catalogued under Juan de Matos Fragoso, the second under 'Tiempo'.

R34 and IT13C; their other types have been associated with Miranda in the lists above. W11 therefore provides a useful link between signed Miranda items and certain Pepys *sueltas*. As a bonus, the *sueltas* of *El imposible mas facil* and *A vn tiempo rey y vassallo* can also be attributed to Miranda. We shall try to date them later.

If we anticipate what we are just about to prove, we can tabulate these types and ornaments in the following groups:

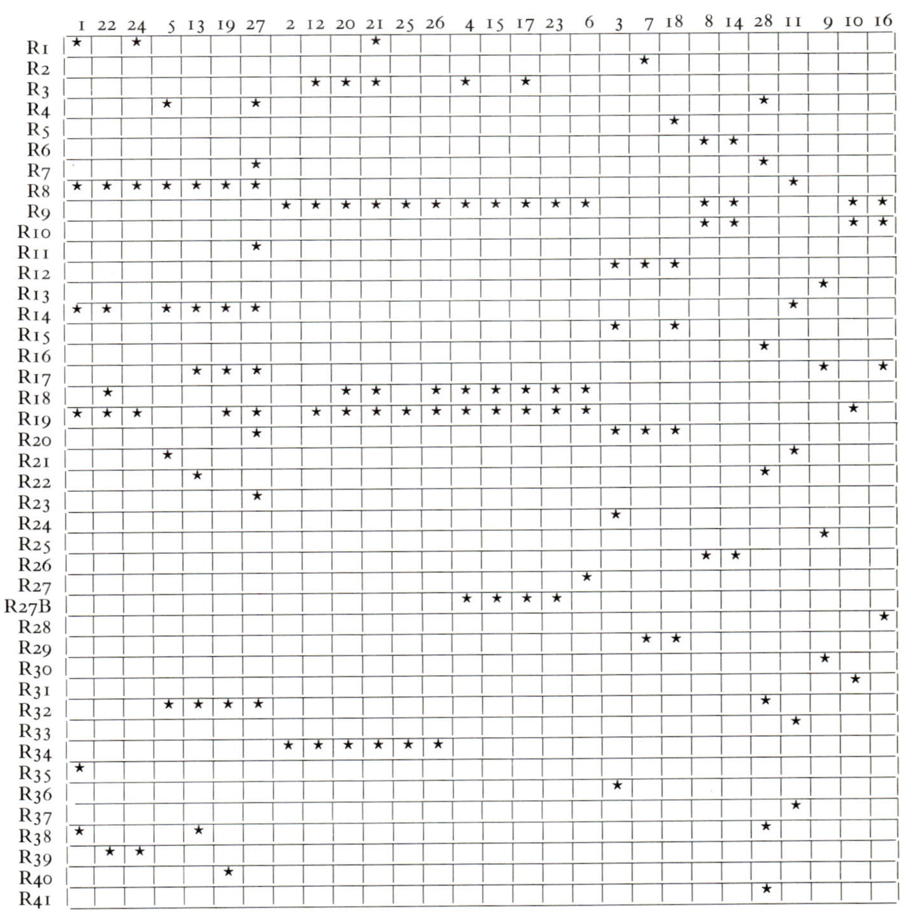

	1	22	24	5	13	19	27	2	12	20	21	25	26	4	15	17	23	6	3	7	18	8	14	28	11	9	10	16
R1	★		★								★																	
R2																				★								
R3									★	★	★			★		★												
R4				★			★																	★				
R5																					★							
R6																						★	★					
R7							★																	★				
R8	★	★	★	★	★	★	★																		★			
R9								★	★	★	★	★	★	★	★	★	★	★				★	★				★	★
R10																						★	★				★	★
R11							★																					
R12																			★	★	★							
R13																										★		
R14	★	★		★	★	★	★																		★			
R15																			★		★							
R16																								★				
R17					★	★	★																			★		★
R18		★								★	★		★	★	★	★	★	★										
R19	★	★	★			★	★		★	★	★	★	★	★	★	★	★	★									★	
R20							★												★	★	★							
R21				★																					★			
R22					★																			★				
R23							★																					
R24																			★									
R25																										★		
R26																						★	★					
R27																		★										
R27B														★	★	★	★											
R28																												★
R29																				★	★							
R30																										★		
R31																											★	
R32				★	★	★	★																	★				
R33																									★			
R34								★	★	★	★	★	★															
R35	★																											
R36																			★									
R37																									★			
R38	★				★																			★				
R39		★	★																									
R40						★																						
R41																								★				

	1	22	24	5	13	19	27	2	12	20	21	25	26	4	15	17	23	6	3	7	18	8	14	28	11	9	10	16
IT1	★					★																		★				
IT2			★	★	★																					★		
IT3		★		★		★	★																					
IT4				★		★	★	★																				
IT5																											★	
IT6	★	★	★			★																		★	★			
IT7																						★	★					
IT8																			★		★							
IT9																										★		
IT10																				★	★							
IT10B		★		★	★	★	★																					
IT10C																									★			
IT11																												★
IT12																											★	
IT13																		★										
IT13B														★	★	★	★											
IT13C								★	★	★	★	★	★															
IT14																			★									
IT15	★																			•								
IT16	★	★	★																									

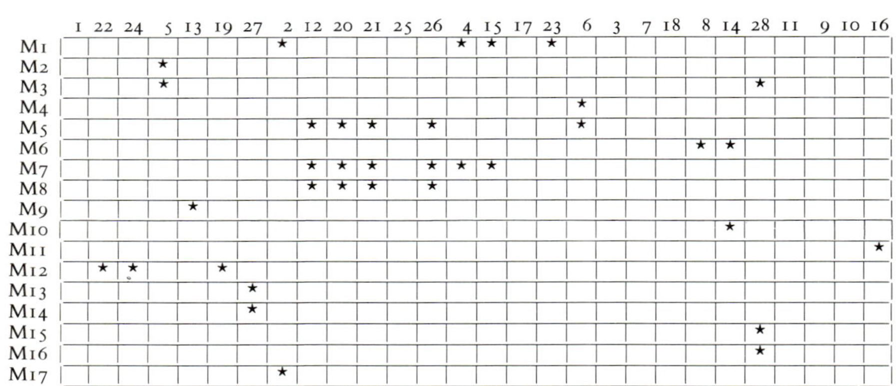

	1	22	24	5	13	19	27	2	12	20	21	25	26	4	15	17	23	6	3	7	18	8	14	28	11	9	10	16
M1								★						★	★		★											
M2				★																								
M3				★																				★				
M4																		★										
M5									★	★	★		★					★										
M6																						★	★					
M7									★	★	★		★	★	★													
M8									★	★	★		★															
M9					★																							
M10																							★					
M11																												★
M12		★	★			★																						
M13							★																					
M14							★																					
M15																								★				
M16																								★				
M17								★																				

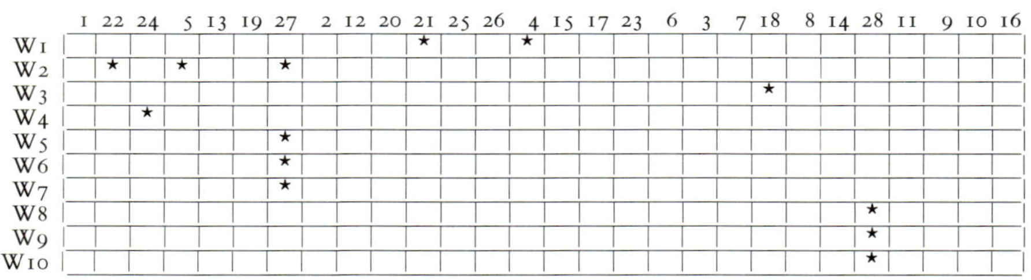

	1	22	24	5	13	19	27	2	12	20	21	25	26	4	15	17	23	6	3	7	18	8	14	28	11	9	10	16
W1											★			★														
W2		★		★			★																					
W3																					★							
W4			★																									
W5							★																					
W6							★																					
W7							★																					
W8																								★				
W9																								★				
W10																								★				

Some groups stand out more clearly than others, but the first seven items are manifestly linked by R8, present in all of them, and also by R14, IT10B, and to a lesser extent by IT3, IT4, IT16, M12 and W2. The next eleven items (from 2 to 6, in the order in which we have put them) appear to be linked by R9, but R9 alone does not exclude 8, 14, 10 or 16. That these four should be excluded seems obvious from R18, R19, M5, M7 and M8. Further examination, particularly of the italics 13, 13B and 13C, but also of the romans 27, 27B and 34, indicates that this large group of eleven should be divided into three sub-groups: 2, 12, 20, 21, 25 and 26 in one; 4, 15, 17 and 23 in another; and 6 by itself in a third. The two larger groups are connected by R9, R18, R19, M1, M7, and even by the wood-block W1, present in 21 and 4. Number 6 is connected more tenuously, by R9, R18, R19, none of them exclusive to this large group, and by M5; however, its roman and italic text-types (R27 and IT13) provide links in terms of typefaces, though the founts are different. That 3, 7 and 18 form yet another group is clear from R12, R15, R20, R29, IT8 and IT10, five of which are found only in these three *sueltas*. The link between 8 and 14 is even more striking: they share no fewer than six of the seven kinds of type and ornaments used in them, four of them found nowhere else. The remaining five items, one *vejamen* and four *sueltas*, will not fit comfortably into any of the preceding groups.

We must emphasise that while the schematic nature of these tables may help the eye to grasp evidence, it conceals a great deal of essential information. Thus *sueltas* 1 and 24 are linked less by the presence in them of R1 (which is also to be found in 21), than by the fact that the same damaged sorts of R1 are found in both; and *sueltas* 8, 14, 10 and 16 ought not to be linked together merely because they all use R9 and R10, for 16 mixes these two faces, whereas R9 is mixed with R6 in 8 and 14. In short, the tables conceal some relationships and imply that others exist which do not. They are no more than a visual guide to the real evidence, which must be extracted from the lists preceding them.

As was pointed out in the article referred to earlier (Chapter I, note 2), some woodblocks used by Miranda were later used by Cabezas, many of whose blocks passed in turn to Vejarano. The lists above suggest very strongly that this was also true of type, and that Cabezas also acquired some of the type of the widow Rodríguez, who apparently stopped printing in 1674–5, just as Cabezas was starting. We believe that in order to print one particularly lavish item, the *Fiestas de la Santa Iglesia Metropolitana . . . de Sevilla* of Fernando de la Torre Farfán (1671), the widow Rodríguez borrowed some typefaces which did not form part of her usual stock; at any rate she used them only in this book. Cabezas, on the other hand, as a result of acquiring typographical material from various sources, had, by Spanish standards, a wealth of it. A glance through the lists above shows that he used, over a period of about seven years, twenty romans, eight italics and nine kinds of metal ornament. Sometimes he had two faces on the same body, and we have seen other typefaces in his books which we have not recorded because they are not used in Pepys 1553. This range of type does not put him in the Plantin class, but it was roughly twice as large as that of most Spanish contemporaries. One consequence of it is that his unsigned work is hard to date accurately: since he apparently started his career with plenty of type, he found less need for periodic replacements. Despite these complications, we feel able to name printers for most of the *sueltas*. We give one example, admittedly a very straightforward one, from *suelta* 3, to show the method in operation.

Types of *suelta* 3 (Tirso, *Los lagos de San Vicente*):

R12: widow Rodríguez (different T) 1671–3, Cabezas (doubtful) 1676–9, López de Haro 1679–83 (as in the *sueltas*).

R15: widow Rodríguez 1673–4, López de Haro 1679–84.

R20: widow Rodríguez 1671–4, Cabezas 1675–8 (worn), López de Haro 1679–83.

R24: López de Haro 1679–83.

R36: López de Haro 1683–4, same body and condition.

IT8: López de Haro 1683.
IT14: López de Haro 1684, same body, same adulteration.
On this evidence it seems quite obvious that *suelta* 3 was printed by López de Haro: he had all seven typefaces at roughly the same time, and several of them were uniquely his. One book in particular, Luis de Valdivia's *Arte, y gramatica general de la lengua que corre en todo el Reyno de la Chile* (López de Haro, 1684), shows the text-types R36 and IT14 in virtually the same state as in the *suelta*. Perhaps they are slightly more worn in Valdivia's book, which suggests that the *suelta* may have been printed in 1683. The attribution is made more convincing by the great rarity of IT14.

In the same way, and making cautious use of cumulative evidence from earlier attributions, we have attributed twenty-four of the twenty-seven imprintless items to the following printers:

1	*El premio en la tirania*	Cabezas, *c.* 1675–8
5	*La creacion del mundo . . .*	Cabezas, *c.* 1676–9
13	*La azuzena de Etiopia*	
19	*El divino portugues . . .*	
27	First *Vejamen*	
22	*El mejor padre de pobres*	Cabezas, *c.* 1678
24	*No ay dicha, ni desdicha . . .*	

No great weight should be attached to our Cabezas guess-dates: they overlap, and it might be argued that we could have ranged all seven items together under the heading *c.* 1675–9, without putting any strain on the accepted meaning of *circa*. However, the guess-dates have the virtue of dividing Cabezas's products into groups. Whether these groups are the result of differences in date, in the preferences of individual compositors, or of other factors, is not clear; but groups there are. The cause of our uncertainty has been mentioned already: Cabezas's large stock of type. Some of his output has assuredly been lost; even if we had seen all that survives (which we have not), it might be hard to discover exactly when each face was in his shop and available to his compositors: it would never be necessary to use all his typefaces to print a single book, no matter how large it was. Occasionally we have managed to follow the fate of a typeface closely: for example, R14 was used by the widow Rodríguez from 1671 to 1674, by Cabezas from 1675 to 1681, and by Vejarano from 1681 to 1683. We can therefore deduce that this was probably a single fount passed from printer to printer; it does not help us to date work printed by Cabezas. The block W2, on the other hand, has been seen to be used by Cabezas only in 1676, and by Vejarano only in 1682. No doubt Cabezas had it in the years 1676 to 1681, but we cannot be certain. However, it is no more helpful for dating purposes than R14: even if it was not observed between 1676 and 1682, it was certainly in existence, and could have been used at any time. It illustrates very well the difficulties posed by Cabezas. We give such evidence as we can.

The text roman (R38) and italic (IT15) of *suelta* 1 were used by Cabezas in a pamphlet dated 1675 (B.L., 811.e.51[11]). Their use as text-types sets *suelta* 1 apart from the others attributable to Cabezas, but since he also used R38 in 1676, and IT16 only (to our knowledge) in 1678, we opt for *c.* 1675–8.

Item 27 (the first *Vejamen*) deals with events of 27 December 1675, and so must have been at press in late 1675 or early 1676. Its use of R32 and IT10B links it with *sueltas* 5, 13 and 19. The body of IT10B cannot be measured in 27, but since R32 is 84 mm/20 lines in all four, we can safely assume that the body of IT10B was 84 mm in 27 as well. Unfortunately, Cabezas used both these text-types from 1676 to 1681. His use of a mixture of IT3 and IT4 (in 5, 19 and 27) can be seen in Francisco de Godoy's *Lo que saliere* (B.L., 12316.g.20) and Diego Cebreros's *Sevilla festiva* (B.L., 486.c.4[2]), both dated 1676, but also as late as 1679 (in Pepys 1545/9/58). For these reasons, we are reluctant to commit ourselves to a date more definite than *c.* 1676–9 for *sueltas* 5, 13 and 19.

Sueltas 22 and 24 are linked by their use of the text-types

R39 and IT16, both used by Cabezas in 1678 (in B.L. pamphlet 1445.f.17[64]). Each *suelta* is decorated with a woodblock (W2 and W4); Cabezas used both these blocks in Cebreros's *Sevilla festiva*. We opt for *c.* 1678 because the other typefaces give no more precise indication.

2	*San Franco de Sena*	Miranda, *c.* 1675
12	*La segunda Magdalena . . .*	
20	*El milagro por los zelos*	
21	*El angel de la guarda*	
25	*Los trabajos de Tobias*	
26	*Santa Maria Egipciaca . . .*	

4	*La sirena del Iordan . . .*	Miranda, *c.* 1678
6	*El esclavo de Maria*	
15	*El condenado por desconfiado*	
17	*El gigante cananeo*	
23	*La obediencia laureada*	

There can be little doubt that Miranda printed these two groups. Woodblock 1, apparently peculiar to Miranda, is found in one *suelta* of each group (4 and 21). The text-types of the first group (R34 and IT13C) appear, along with another woodblock of his, in two imprintless *sueltas*, as we have stated already. The capitals of this wretched roman text-type are found in a pamphlet bearing his imprint (B.L., 811.e.51[15]), and the date 1675. For this reason we date the first group *c.* 1675. If this is correct, the imprintless *sueltas* of *El imposible mas facil* and *A vn tiempo rey y vassallo* must also have been printed by Miranda about 1675. The first, said to be by Calderón in the *suelta* but probably by Matos Fragoso, is attributed to 'Valencia? 1720?' in the British Library catalogue. The second, said to be by three wits (Luis de Belmonte Bermúdez, Manuel Antonio de Vargas and another?) is apparently accepted as part of an authentic copy of *Escogidas VI*.

We date the second group of *sueltas* principally by R27B, used by Miranda in 1678 (B.L., 811.e.51[32]). We have no recorded use *with an imprint* of IT13 in any of its three body-sizes (including IT13B and C), but it is found only in these eleven *sueltas* (thirteen including *El imposible mas facil* and *A vn tiempo rey y vassallo*). We believe that Miranda had matrices for this face, and cast it in three different moulds. We think that he also had matrices for R27 and that the differing body-sizes of R27 and R27B can be explained in this way. We do not suggest that Miranda cast type for other printers, merely that he had managed to acquire two ancient and adulterated sets of text-type matrices, and that he had sufficient skill as a metal-worker to cast type in them and, perhaps, to make his own moulds. His skill as a metal- and wood-worker is borne out by his two signed copper engravings and the signed wood-cut (see above, Chapter II). As we said earlier, *suelta* 6, with the different body-size of its text-type, does not obviously belong to either group. We have put it in the second group, however, partly because of the connection between R27 and R27B, partly because two of its other typefaces were used by Miranda in 1678; but if R27B is to be thought of as an improved version of R27, then 6 must be earlier than the other four in the group.

3 *Los lagos de San Vicente* } López de Haro, *c.* 1683

7 *El premio de la virtud . . .*
18 *El animal profeta . . .* } López de Haro, *c.* 1678–83

Suelta 3 has been dealt with above. We think 7 and 18 are earlier, but we have not seen enough items printed in the period 1678–83 to be more precise.

8 *La aurora del sol divino*
14 *El mejor rey del mundo . . .* } J. F. de Blas, *c.* 1673

28 Second *Vejamen* } signed J. F. de Blas 1682

The principal evidence for the date of 8 and 14 and for their attribution to J. F. de Blas is Francisco de Florencia's *Exemplar vida, y gloriosa muerte . . . del . . . padre Luis de Medina* (B.L., 1232.c.6), which Blas printed in 1673 and which contains all the typefaces used in the *sueltas*, in a similar condition and degree of adulteration. By 1682 Blas had a rather different stock of type, but there seems to be no reason to doubt that he printed 28, especially since he appears to have been the owner of woodblock 8, used by him in Fernando de Escaño's *Tractatus de perfectione voluntatis* of 1676 (B.L., 5322.ee.7). One reason for Blas's different stock of type seems to have been the acquisition, in 1682, of part of the stock of Cabezas, who stopped printing in 1681. A total of eight faces (R7, R22, R32, R38, IT1, IT6, M3 and M15) which had been used by Cabezas were used by Blas from 1682. Six of those faces (i.e. all but R7 and M3) also appear in the work of Vejarano. As we suggested in Chapter II, the output of Vejarano did not match that of his predecessor Cabezas. We suspect that he ran a more modest business altogether, and that as part of this policy he (or Hermosilla) sold off part of Cabezas's large stock of type: not whole founts, but portions of them, retaining the rest for himself. Thus Vejarano seems to have kept part of the fount of Granjon's *ascendonica cursive,* while part was acquired by Blas, who used it in item 28 and in Juan de Rioja's *Sermon funebre . . . a . . . d. Antonio de Lemos* of 1683 (B.L., 4865.dd.20[13]). Part of the fount (Vejarano's share?) seems eventually to have fallen into the hands of Antonio Román of Madrid, who used it from 1685 to 1692, eking it out with the face cut by Guyot for the same body.[61]

11 *El juramento ante Dios . . .* } widow Rodríguez, 1671–4

Of the seven typefaces in this *suelta*, five were used by the widow and by Cabezas. This leads us to believe the Cabezas acquired some of the widow's type about 1674, as was suggested above. The remaining two faces, R33 and R37, are found only in the widow's books. Moreover, *suelta* 11 is better printed than the others, and is distinctly reminiscent of the

[61] See Cruickshank, 'Some aspects of Spanish book-production in the Golden Age', *The Library*, V, xxxi (1976), 17, n. 66. Also Antonio de Solís y Rivadeneira, *Varias poesias*, Madrid, Antonio Román, 1692 (B.L., 686.g.25).

high standards (for the time) which she displayed in Torre Farfán's *Fiestas* of 1671.

The three *sueltas* still unaccounted for are 9, 10 and 16. Their typographical details are as follows:

Suelta 9 (Calderón, *La exaltacion de la Cruz*)

R13: Miranda 1671, heirs of J. G. de Blas 1678.
R17: widow Rodríguez 1671, J. F. de Blas 1669–76, Cabezas 1674–80, Ramos 1676, Ossuna 1681, Vejarano 1681–3.
R25: no user recorded.
R30: Miranda 1671.
IT2: J. F. de Blas 1672–6, Cabezas 1674–80, heirs of J. G. de Blas 1678, Vejarano 1683.
IT9: Miranda 1671.

The evidence favours Miranda, who used the text-types R30 and IT9 in 1671 (B.L., 1323.g.1[13]). The lack of evidence for his use of R25 and IT2 is not unusual; nor would it be unusual to find that he used R17 (Granjon's *parangon romain*) only in this *suelta*, except that he definitely had Garamont's *parangonne romaine* (R18), i.e. a different design of the same size of type. On the other hand, as the lists above show, it was not exceptional for a printer to have two different designs for the same body. More evidence is needed for confirmation, but on the basis of that at present available, Miranda is the most likely printer of this *suelta*, about 1671. In any event it must have been printed in Seville *c.* 1670–80.

Suelta 16 (Olivares, *Guardar palabra a los santos*)

R9: widow Rodríguez 1671, Ossuna 1671–81, J. F. de Blas 1673–6, Miranda 1675–8, Cabezas 1678, Vejarano 1682.
R10: widow Rodríguez 1671, Miranda 1671, J. F. de Blas 1669–76.
R17: widow Rodríguez 1671, J. F. de Blas 1669–76, Cabezas 1674–80, Ramos 1676, Ossuna 1681, Vejarano 1681–3.
R28: J. F. de Blas 1672 (correct body-size, but lacking two-dot j); Miranda had a few sorts in 1671, including the j,

but on an 86 mm body, not 85, although this could be accounted for by variable paper-shrinkage.

IT11: López de Haro 1683.

M11: J. G. de Blas 1639.

The most likely candidates for this *suelta* are Miranda (1671?) and J. F. de Blas (1672?). If Miranda *did* print *suelta* 9 about 1671, then he had R17, which increases the odds in his favour. R9 and R10 are mixed in the *suelta*, and J. F. de Blas often mixed R9 – but mixed it with R6. This evidence could be taken as against or in favour of his involvement. M11, being an ornament, could easily have survived thirty years and have been passed from father to son, but nothing is proved by it. On present evidence we are reluctant to choose between Miranda and Blas, but we feel reasonably sure that the *suelta* was printed in Seville round about 1670.

Suelta 10 (Calderón, *Las cadenas del demonio*)

R9: widow Rodríguez 1671, Ossuna 1671–81, J. F. de Blas 1673–6, Miranda 1675–8, Cabezas 1678, Vejarano 1682.

R10: widow Rodríguez 1671, Miranda 1671, J. F. de Blas 1669–76.

R19: Miranda 1675–8, Cabezas 1675–81, J. F. de Blas 1676–7, heirs of J. G. de Blas 1678, Ossuna 1680–1, Vejarano 1682–3.

R31: no user recorded.

IT5: no user recorded.

IT12: no user recorded in Seville.

We do not know who printed this *suelta*. Its use of R9, R10 and R19 is of little significance, for all three of these faces were common in Spain (and in Europe) throughout the seventeenth century. One piece of useful (but so far inconclusive) evidence is that it is signed on all four leaves of each gathering (i.e. A, A2, A3, A4, etc.). We have never seen this feature in seventeenth-century Madrid printing. Such examples as we have seen are not signed, but some of them can be associated, directly or indirectly, with Seville. For example, two *sueltas* with this feature are found in the made-up volume entitled *Doze comedias nuevas de diferentes autores, parte XXXXXVII* [sic], Valencia, 1646. Restori, who describes this volume, argues plausibly that the two preliminary leaves were printed in Seville in the late seventeenth century, possibly by the firm later run by Francisco de Leefdael, who printed there in the early part of the eighteenth century.[62] We have also seen multiple signatures (rather irregular ones) in one of the *sueltas* in the Pennsylvania collection (Francisco de Rojas Zorrilla, *El prodigio def* [sic] *Arabia*).[63] We suspect that several of the *sueltas* bound in the same volume were printed in Seville, and that the one with the multiple signatures was the work of Tomé de Dios Miranda (*c.* 1675). Restori points out that the two *sueltas* in the 'Valencia' volume appear to come from different printing-houses, and since we have no typographical reason to associate Miranda with Pepys 1553(10), we believe that the multiple signatures may not be an example of what would now be called 'house style', but perhaps the hallmark of a few compositors employed in the Seville area in the middle of the second half of the seventeenth century. We think in terms of more than one compositor because we know of two copies of another edition of Pepys 1553 (10) (described below, p. 142), which, although printed in the same type (and therefore by the same firm), reveal sufficient differences in spelling to suggest

[62] A. Restori, *Saggi di bibliografia teatrale spagnuola*, Geneva, 1927, pp. 1–10.
[63] J.M. Regueiro, *A catalogue of the comedia collection in the University of Pennsylvania Libraries*, New Haven (Connecticut), 1971, no. 664. [Since discovering the importance of W11 (p. 56 above), I have managed to re-examine the film of the volume containing this *suelta*. No. 659 is another copy of *El imposible mas facil*; no. 665, *El hijo de las batallas*, also uses W11 as a tailpiece; no. 658, *El piadoso Aragones*, from its type, is Miranda's work; for 667, *El esclavo de Maria*, see our *suelta* 6 description below. No. 660, *En el engaño el remedio*, is by Juan Francisco de Blas, with his block W8, and seems contemporary with our *sueltas* 8 and 14; and type suggests that Blas was the printer of no. 663, *El embuste acreditado*. These discoveries affect (marginally) our figures for production of ephemera in Seville; but many more such discoveries are simply waiting to be made – D.W.C.]

the involvement of another compositor. In the circumstances we feel that the most ambitious guess that can be made for *suelta* 10 is Seville? 1650–84. If its unusual text-types turn up in a signed item, then it should be possible to date it more accurately and to assign it to its printer with some confidence.

Apart from giving us an idea of the relative textual importance of these *sueltas*, this exercise in dating provides us with an additional glimpse of the book trade in Seville. The average date of the twenty-five 'dated' items (excluding, that is, numbers 9, 10 and 16) is 1677. A few of them were more than ten years old when Pepys bought them, and most of them were probably at least five years old. So perhaps these rather ephemeral productions did not enjoy the quick sale that their appearance might lead us to expect. The attributions to the various printers do not greatly affect what we said earlier about their output, with the exception of Miranda. In Chapter II we remarked that we knew of only twenty-one items with his imprint, and attributed three more to him. In this chapter we have attributed eleven Pepys *sueltas* and three other *sueltas* to him, and named him as the printer most likely to have produced Pepys 1553(9). The attributable items therefore total eighteen, an increase of eighty-six per cent in terms of items, although the increase is composed entirely of ephemera. From what we have seen, we think there are many more *suelta* editions waiting to be attributed to Miranda, and that he must have been one of the busiest producers of *sueltas* in Seville. As we shall see in Chapter V, he also had a rather bad record for giving the correct names of the authors of the plays he printed. It might be instructive to investigate the *suelta* texts he produced from the viewpoint of fidelity to copy, but this is not the place for such an exercise.

The firm attribution of all but one of the items (10) to Seville printers is also of interest. Since Pepys is unlikely to have concentrated on buying specifically Seville printing (he could scarcely have known that the *sueltas* were Seville work unless he had been told), it would seem that the stocks of Seville booksellers consisted mainly of local printing. This is corroborated by Pepys volume 1545, in which the great majority of signed or attributable items are also Seville work. The two Pepys volumes are a very small sample, but they help to confirm the picture of a depressed provincial printing industry which produced large quantities of ephemeral material for the local market. In addition they suggest, by their apparently slow rate of sale, that the local market was not a very lively one.

COMEDIA

R1

COMEDIA

R2

COMEDIA

R3

COMEDIA

R4

COMEDIA

R5

COMEDIA FAMOSA

R6 [note foreign (R9) O and E in COMEDIA]

FRANCISCO

R7

COMEDIA FAMOSA

R8 [note damaged M in COMEDIA]

FAMOSA:

R9

COMEDIA FAMOSA.

R10 (note F, A . . . A from R9)

CON QVE SE AFECTO

R11

EL ANIMAL PROFETA.

R12

IORNADA PRIMERA.

R13

LA CREACION DEL MVNDO,
y primera culpa del hombre.

R14

L O S L A G O S

R15

EL SEÑOR DON JVAN BEXINES

R16

DE LA EXALTACION DE LA CRVZ.

R17

EL ESCLAVO DE MARIA.

R18

DE DON PEDRO CALDERON.

R19 (note foreign L)

A C T O P R I M E R O.

R20

DEL ALFEREZ JACINTO CORDERO.

R21 (the small caps)
(the C in JACINTO is foreign)

gayta Gallegá; tercero (porq̃ diferencien) se les sacará a Dulcinea del Toboso, porq̃ en esto de regalar, me precio de Quixote; porque no falten xicaras en que darlas el chocolate, he imbiado a castilla, por vn lugar que llaman Cienpoçuelos; tambien repartire entre todas algunos dones, y no serán de los postizos que se vsan aora, sino los Dones del Espiritu Santo, que las lleve a descançar, quanto antes, y en particular a las que se hallaren suegras. Ea su Magestad las encamine; vayan con Dios, y no gruñan, que bien regaladas van.

R22

IORNADA PRIMERA.

de MARIA, claro està
que el mejor hombre ser à
del mundo, y el mas dichoso.
Ami. Con justa razon suspendes
en este himeneo el alma.
Lis. Que mas venturosa palma?
Ami. En dulce fuego te enciendes.

R23/R26

PERSONAS.

R24

DE DON PEDRO

R25

pues tambien dezirla saves.
Que saben los Cielos bien,
que ha sido mi casamiento
sin gusto del pensamiento,
porque estava puesto en quiẽ,
y a mi verguença lo dize:
corrida estoy. *d. Iu.* Yo turbado
y amante, al fin he pensado
A que

R27

de sde esse incassible
trono es luz hermoso, aqui e sirviẽdo
estàn Angeles bellos,
mas que la luz del sol, ermosos ellos
Mil glorias quiero daros (do
por las mercedes q̃ me estais haziẽ-
sin sabar obligaros,
quando yo mereci, que del estruendo

R27B

IORNADA PRIMERA.
la ſentencia criminal;
ni es punto,con mas razon,
el que vn ſecreto ha fiado
de vn amigo, y rebelado
le oye en converſacion;
ni admiracion ſemejante,

R28 (note foreign j)

tengo de quemar la cama,
donde eſtuvo el perro ruzio.
Cie. Bien haràs. *Bul.* No sè que diera
por averle echado al punto
entonces la melecina.
Iul. Ea amigos,todos juntos
emos de dar a Dios gracias
deſte bien: luzes al punto
ſacad,y en la Igleſia entremos.
Lau. Agradecimiento es juſto.

R29

*Sir.*Hà del ſoberuio monte,
que linea deſigual deſte Orizonte,
tanto à los cielos ſube,
que vna vez es montaña,y otra nube.
*Men.*Hà de las altas peñas,
que confundiendo equiuocas las ſeñas,
de luzes, y verdores,
vna vez ſois eſtrellas,y otras flores.
*Sir.*Hà del ruſtico ſeno,.

R30

Que delito cometi
contra voſotros naciendo,
que fue de vn ſepulcro a otro
paſſar no mas,quando veo
que la fiera,el pez,y el aue
gozan de los priuilegios
del nacer,ſiendo ſu eſtancia
la tierra,el agua,y el viento?
A que fin,Dioſes,echaſteis
a mal en mi nacimiento

R31

Eſcuchad, atended,
admirados,ſuſpenſos,
en ſola vna palabra,
ſin voz,muchos conceptos.
El Rey mas ſoberano
que ſaludais atentes,
ſin mudar ſitio,viene

R32

muchas vitorias te he dado,
no es la primera Rey eſta.
Efetos ſon de vn dolor
los anuncios deſta pena,
y es la mia tan mortal,
que pido á vueſtra grandeza,
no me pregunte la cauſa.

R33

llamadme zeloſo amante.
*Criſp.*Señor amor, porque eſtâ
tan zeloſo? que gran pena
con tantos zelos nos dâ.
*Ceſ.*Si ſe casô. Magdalena,
que vida me queda ya?
*Criſ.*Iamas he de ſer criado

R34 (note M)

JORNADA PRIMERA.

R35 (small caps)

no doy por bueſo cogote
vn piro. *Fer.* Que ſierra es eſta?
Paſ. La Bureba de Caſtilla.
Fer. Notables riſcos! *Paſ.* Mancilla
vos tengo. *Fer.* Que eſtraña cueſta!
Paſ. Llamaſe eſpanta roines.
Fer. No ſe yo, que aya en Eſpaña
tan eſcabroſa montaña.
Paſ. Mala es para con chapines.

R36

Y LEALTAD CONTRA EL AMOR.

R37 (small caps)

Conſt. TIrana crueldad, qué intentas?
Reſolucion del deſſeo,
què pretendes? Lucha cruel
del agonal penſamiento,

R38

que con vn alma tenemos;
Don Ordoño, y Don Garcia
hijos legitimos ſon
de Alfonſo, Rey de Leon,
y pretenden eſte dia
ambos el Reyno, y alegan,
que Don Garcia es mayor;
Don Ordoño, que al traydor
las Chriſtianas leyes niegan

R39

JORNADA PRIMERA.

R40 (small caps)

PEDRO DE SANTIAGO

R41 (small caps)

Por Don Franciſco Balcarcel y Lugo.

IT1

DE D.FRANCISCO DE LA TORRE.

IT2

San Miguel.	*Eva.*	*Lamech.*
Luzbel.	*Cain.*	*Iubal.*
Adan.	*Abel.*	*Seth.*

IT3 (note IT4 sorts, e.g. *M*)

DE DON AGVSTIN MORETO.

IT4

DE DON PEDRO CALDERON.

IT5

Conſtantino Emperador.	*Roſimunda, Princeſa de Bohemia.*
Feliſardo ſu primo.	*Roſaura, criada.*
Caliſto, Priuado.	*Leonardo, Capitan de la guardia.*
Eſteuan, Anacoreta.	*Jorge, gracioſo. Tres Pages.*
Polidoro, Rey de Hungria, barba.	*Claudiano, General.*
Florencia, Monja.	*Acompañamiento.*

IT6

El Rey David.
La Reyna Bersabè.
El Rey Salomon.
Bañ..ias Capitan.
Az..rias Capitan.
Sadoc Sacerdote.
El pueblo.
Momo pastor.
Vn Egipcio Embaxador.
Arminda.
Abisac.
Vna Vision.
Dos ciudadanos.
Vn Secretario.
Vn Piloto.
Vn Angel.
Musica.
Soldados.

IT7

El Animal Profeta.

IT8

Salen Siroes, y Menardes, Principes de Persia, cada vno por su puerta, representando al teatro, que ha de ser vna montana.

IT9

El Rey de Dinamarca el viejo.
El Conde Vitorino.
La Duquesa Rosaura su hermana.
Beatriz criada. Perele gracioso.
La Infana Lenia.
Elvira Dama.
Felino Principe de Albania.
Silvio, y Cipido criados.

IT10 (also 10B, 10C)

Casimiro galan.
Leonido galan.
Aurelio viejo.
Faustino niño.
Eufemia dama.
Celia Dama.
Marcela criada.
Arista, y Fabio criados.

IT11

San Bartolome.
El Rey.
Licandro.
Ceusis.
El Demonio.
Vn Sacerdote.
Yrene.
Siluia.
Flora.
Lesbia.
Liron.
Criados.

IT12

Don Iuan.
Gaznate, gracioſo.
Laura, dama.
Olaya, Criada.
Leonardo galan.
Celio galan.

Don Lope, barba.
Feniſa, dama.
El Duque de Albur-
querque.
Soldados de guarda.
Calonge, ventero.

Tallaſero. Vandolero.
Vn Rufian.
Vn Vegete.
Vn Correo.
Vn moço de mulas.
Y algunos caminantes.

IT13 (note foreign *v*)

Paulo Ermitaño.
Pedriſco gracioſo.
El Demonio.
Otavio, y Liſardo.

Celia, y Lidora criada.
Enrico.
Galvan, y Eſcalante.
Roldan. Cherino.

Anareto padre de Enrico. Vn Alcalde
Albano viejo. Vn portero. Vn Iuez.
Vn Paſtor. Vn Muſico.
Vn Governador. Algunos villanos.

IT13B (note foreign *v*, misaligned)

El Rey don Iuan el Segundo.
Don Alvaro de Luna.
La Reyna Doña Iſabel de
Portugal.
Doña Beatriz de Silva.

Don Iuan de Silva ſu tio.
Silveyra lacayo.
Vn gentilhombre.
Leonor villana.
Muſicos.

IT13C (note foreign *v* and *z*)

Paſqual Ruſtico.
Fernando Rey.
Don Tello.
Doña Blanca.
Dos Cautiuos.

Axa Mora.
Rey Moro.
Carraſco Paſtor.
Mari Pablos.
Muſicos.

Ali Petràn Moro.
Dos Moros.
Don Gutierre.
Don Garcia.
Caſilda Santa.

San Vicente.
Auen Rogel, Moro.
Nueſtra Señora.
Iuan Paſqual.
Dos Paſtores.

En lo alto de vnos riſcos Paſqual villano muy à lo groſſero con vn baſton, y vna honda.
Por la mitad de los riſcos el Rey Don Fernando de caza.

IT14

Correſe vna cortina, y aparece Conſtantino
ſentado en vna ſilla, fojeando libros, que
eſtaràn ſobre vn bufete.

IT15

El Rey Don Garcia.
El Rey Don Ordoño.
Don Diego de Porzelos.
Don Uela.

Mongana, gracioſo.
Carraſco, gracioſo.
Soldados.

Doña Violante, Reyna.
Doña Leonor.
Brianda, Eſclava.

IT16 (note foreign *U* and roman ñ)

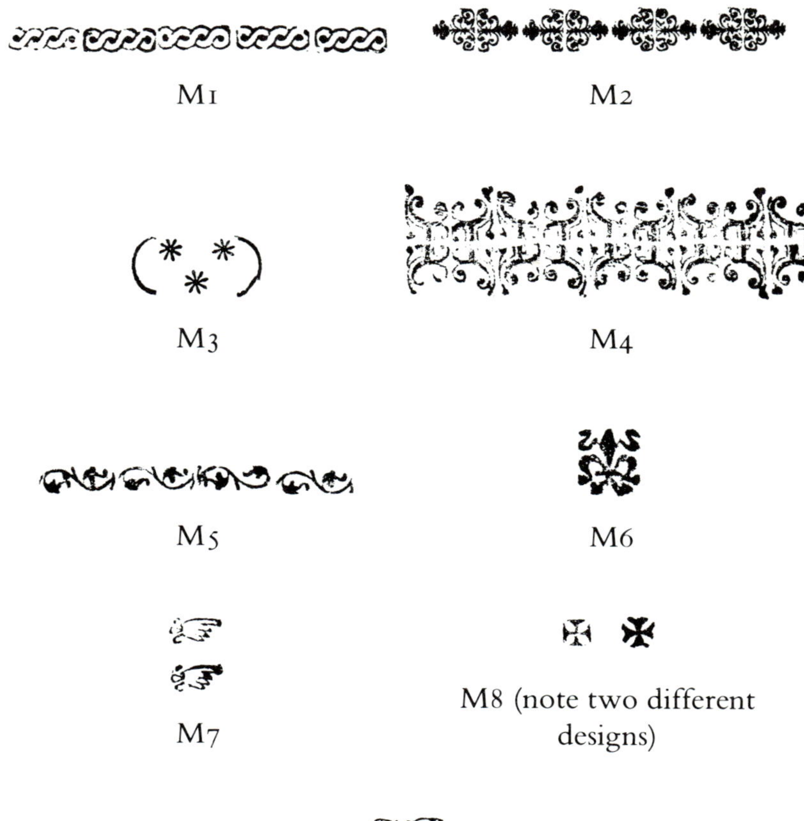

M1

M2

M3

M4

M5

M6

M7

M8 (note two different designs)

M9

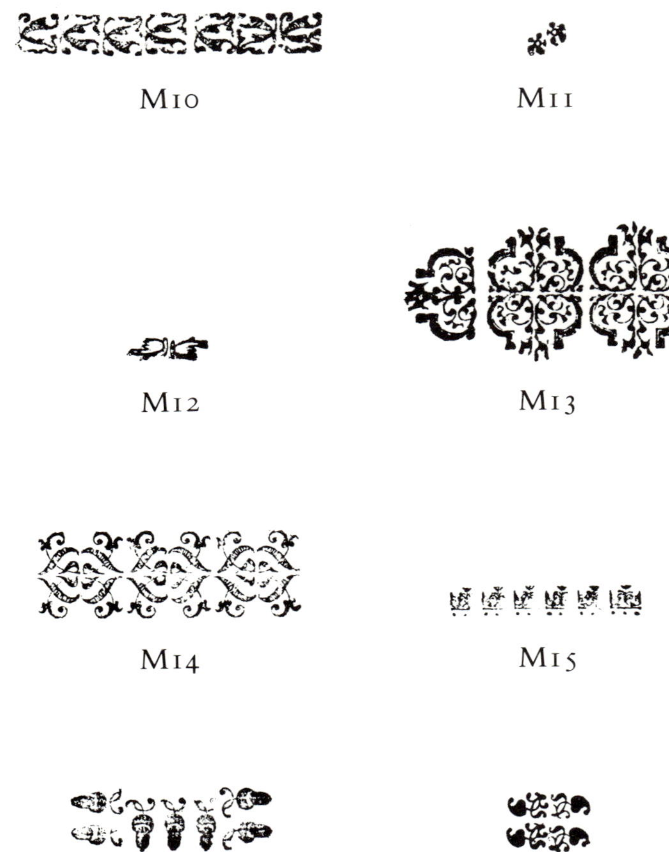

M10

M11

M12

M13

M14

M15

M16

M17

W1

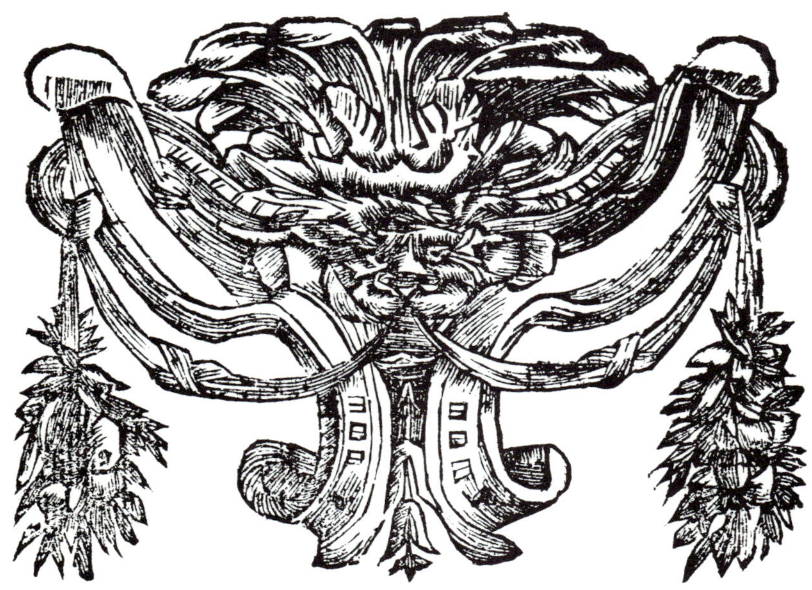

W2

W3

W4

W5

W6

W7

W8

W9 W10

W11 (reproduced by permission of the British Library).

CHAPTER FOUR

The comedia suelta: *History of a Format*

WE have already defined roughly the meaning of *comedias sueltas* in the opening paragraph of our first chapter. The descriptions that follow this one will show the characteristics of those bought by Pepys in Seville in 1684. No one has yet tried to write a historical account of the printing of Spanish plays; perhaps these notes will give bibliographers an indication of it. We shall first outline the main features of the Pepys plays. Twenty-two of them are in four gatherings, three in five, and one (an authentic play of Calderón's) in six. Those in five gatherings take up only four and a half sheets; one of those in four takes up three and a half sheets. A few have typographical ornaments or woodblocks, but none has figurines such as can be found in some earlier specimens. There are no title-pages in them, only head-titles and running headlines. The octosyllabic lines are invariably in double columns, but the passages in eleven-syllable lines are sometimes in a single column, centrally spaced. None has either imprint or date. Most of them consist of one play only, but no. 1 has a short complimentary poem on the last page, and no. 5, which contains a shorter play, is completed by a *Loa sacramental* (a prologue about the Sacrament) on the last two leaves.

Any historical account of the evolution of the *comedia suelta* must take into account not only the ways in which a number of different plays were printed in one volume but also the development of the literary form of the plays in themselves. In the early period (say, up to 1550) the longer plays often had no sense of fitting into a prescribed number of acts, though sometimes there is a pause in speech and in action towards the middle of them. The first plays to be printed were by Juan del Encina (b. Salamanca, 1468; d. León, *c.* 1529), the reputed father of the Spanish theatre; his earliest *égloga* was acted in the Duke of Alba's palace in 1492. Encina's beautifully printed *Cancionero* appeared in Salamanca in 1496; it is a folio which after the preliminaries collates a–s^6 t–v^4. The main body of the book contains his *ars poetica*, poems religious and profane, as well as his Spanish adaptations of Virgil's *Eclogues*; his own eight *églogas* begin on leaf $s1^r$ and end on $v4^r$. We may note in passing that some of the eclogues are paired: in the first the shepherds called Matthew and John quarrel with one another; in the second two others, Mark and Luke, join them and all four depart to worship at the stable at Bethlehem. Each of these *églogas* consists of 180 lines, but the second ends with a carol (*villancico*) of 80 additional lines. The *Cancionero* was reprinted at Seville (Pegnitzer and Herbst) in 1501, at Burgos (Andrés de Burgos), 1505, at Salamanca (Hans Gysser), 1507 and 1509, and at Saragossa (no copy known), 1512 and (by Jorge Coci) 1516. Two additional playlets were added to the edition of 1507. We know of no other plays in Spanish printed in the fifteenth century.[1]

Thanks to the accurate and painstaking researches of Mr F. J. Norton we now know a great deal about peninsular book-production during the postincunabular period (1501–20).[2] At about the turn of the century the Spanish printers began to print works – usually for a relatively humble public – in a single quarto gathering; these productions were soon dubbed *pliegos sueltos*, literally separate or loose gatherings, which some British scholars have translated as chap-books. Spanish scholars sometimes include under this heading some works in two or

[1] The 1496 edition was reproduced in facsimile by the Royal Spanish Academy, with a preface by Emilio Cotarelo y Mori, Madrid, 1928.

[2] Mr Norton has kindly allowed us to use the findings shortly to be published in his *A descriptive catalogue of printing in Spain and Portugal: 1501–1520*, Cambridge, 1978. We are most grateful for his help. We refer to his numbering in the pages that follow in the form N. and the number in round brackets.

even three gatherings, but there is perhaps a danger here of blurring the distinction between a *pliego suelto* and a short book. Often enough these *pliegos* were imprintless and undated. Probably the earliest of these works is a complaint by a man about his servant who, besides being a fortune-teller, is also an idler, a liar, a glutton and one who steals one farthing from every three of his master's spent at the market (N. 236). Mr Norton has identified the printer as Fadrique de Basilea of Burgos and has dated the print as of *c.* 1500–05. Here, then, was a convenient means of popularizing single short dramatic works such as Encina had collected together in his 1496 *Cancionero*.[3]

Plays printed in this format lagged behind the earliest verse chap-books. A few occur towards the end of the postincunabular period. A *pliego suelto* could, of course, contain more than the regular number of four leaves. It was easy to print quartos in eights, in twelves and in sixteens, etc., provided that the preliminary casting-off had been accurately carried out. Mr Norton has described these works in this category:

Juan del Encina, Egloga . . . en la qual representa el Amor . . . a4. [Burgos, Fadrique de Basilea, *c.* 1515–19] (N. 302).

Pero López Ranjel, Farça a honor del nascimiento de nuestro redemptor . . . a4. [Burgos, Alonso de Melgar, *c.* 1520?] (N. 339).

Juan del Encina, Egloga representada en la noche postrera de carnal . . . 4 leaves, no signatures. [Seville, Jacobo Cromberger, *c.* 1515?] (N. 882).

Egloga interlocutoria en la qual se introduzen tres pastores y una zagala . . . a4. [Seville, Jacobo Cromberger, *c.* 1520] (N. 945).

All the plays just mentioned begin with a head-title, and the text immediately follows it; none has a title-page. There is at

[3] See Antonio Rodríguez-Moñino, *Diccionario de pliegos sueltos poéticos – siglo XVI*, Madrid, 1970. Also F. J. Norton and E. M. Wilson, *Two Spanish verse chap-books*, Cambridge, 1969.

least one early example of four plays printed in one bulky gathering:

Alfonso de Castrillo, Tres passos de la Passion y una egloga de la Resurecion. 4°. a^{12}. Burgos, Alonso de Melgar, 1520 (N. 326).

The first leaf was missing from the volume when Joseph Gillet transcribed it. The volume itself has now disappeared from the Biblioteca Menéndez y Pelayo at Santander. Fortunately Gillet's text was printed in the *Publications of the Modern Language Society of America* in 1932.

Other editions of single plays in more than one gathering are to be found before 1521. These, we may suspect, were aimed at a more cultivated and probably wealthier public. Two translations of the *Amphitryon* of Plautus, one by Francisco López de Villalobos, the other by Fernán Pérez de Oliva, were printed respectively by Arnao Guillén de Brocar at Alcalá de Henares in 1517 and (probably) by Juan Varela de Salamanca in Seville, *c.* 1520(?). Both are quartos, and both have title-pages. They collate (again respectively) $a–e^{8}$ and a^{8} b^{12} (N. 51 and N. 1001). As early as 1502–04 Diego Guillén de Ávila's *Egloga interlocutoria*, accompanied by the most shameless of Rodrigo de Reynosa's poems, came out in the types of Stanislao Polono of Alcalá (N. 8). It collates $a–b^{8}$ c^{2}. Perhaps the most famous, and certainly the longest, of Encina's plays (first acted in Rome in 1513), the *Egloga de Placida y Vitoriano*, also without imprint or date, appeared in the types of Alonso de Melgar of Burgos, *c.* 1518–20 (N. 331). Collation: $a–b^{8}$ c^{4}.

There were also three important editions of collected works of dramatists or poet-dramatists printed during these early years. Lucas Fernández, who had been Encina's rival dramatist and musician, had his *Farsas y eglogas* printed in a handsome folio at Salamanca by Lorenzo de Liomdedei in 1514 (N. 571).[4] The collation A^{6} B^{4} C^{6} D^{4} F^{4} a^{6} perhaps indicates that the play in the last gathering went to press at a different time from those

[4] Reproduced in facsimile by the Royal Spanish Academy, Madrid, 1929.

printed in the first five. Each gathering is complete in itself, except that the title-page ($A1^r$) was clearly intended for more than the two items contained in gathering A; and only the last gathering contains a colophon with an imprint (on $a6^r$, verso blank). Gathering E is absent in both copies known to Mr Norton; it may have existed, or may at least have been planned, as may other gatherings between F and a. The printing of the plays was probably conceived of as a collected edition, but since the last five gatherings *could* have been sold separately (each has the author's name at the top of the first page), this may be the earliest collection to merit the title *desglosable* (i.e. 'disbindable', quired in such a way that individual items could be sold separately or together).

The first edition of Pedro Manuel de Urrea's *Cancionero* (collation π^2 a^8 b–h^6, a folio) was printed at Logroño by Arnao Guillén de Brocar in 1513. It contained much poetry and a short play based on the *Celestina* (N. 420). The second edition, also a folio, contained four additional secular plays and one religious one. Juan de Villaquirán of Toledo printed it in 1516 (N. 1122). These works, and those of Lucas Fernández, though pleasing in themselves, had little general influence on the development of Spanish drama; this was not true of those of Torres Naharro.

Bartolomé de Torres Naharro – ?1485–?1520 – (his dates are uncertain) wrote nine plays, eight of which were probably first acted in Italy (Rome and Naples) during the years ?1508–?20. The first edition of his works (up to that date) came out in Naples, printed by Joan Pasquet de Sallo, in 1517.[5] The book was entitled *Propalladia*, and in the *Prohemio* to this volume he explained that this word meant his first offering to Pallas. He

[5] Here and in the following pages we have drawn extensively on the edition in four volumes of *Propalladia and other works of Bartolomé de Torres Naharro*, edited by Joseph E. Gillet, Bryn Mawr and Philadelphia, 1943–61 (the last volume completed by Otis H. Green). Pages 1–128 of the first volume contain Gillet's important bibliographical study of Torres; we refer to the different editions by the letter G. and the number in round brackets.

also explained that the book was ordered in the form of a banquet: it will begin with an *hors-d'oeuvre* of poems and poetic discourses, go on with the principal dishes (the plays) and end with a dessert of shorter poems. Except for his Christmas play, probably an early work, the plays consist of an 'introit', a poetic summary of the plot and five acts; they were influenced by classical and Italian comedies, in form and in subject-matter. The plays vary in length, but one (at least) exceeds 3000 lines, which was about the length of many *comedias* of the Golden Age. Here were great innovations, and not surprisingly Torres Naharro's dramatic powers ensured his continued popularity for the next thirty years.

The first Naples edition of the *Propalladia* contained only seven plays, including the early Christmas one. Ferdinand Columbus, Christopher's bastard son, biographer of his father and benefactor of the Columbina Library at Seville, bought in Valladolid, on 13 November, 1524, a now lost Spanish reprint of the edition of 1517. It cost him 75 *maravedís*. Fortunately he left us a pretty full description of that book, in which he says that it was 'Imp. hispali anno .1520. 20. Junii'. Mr Norton suggests that it may have been printed by Jacobo Cromberger (N. 930). There were later Italian reprints, listed carefully by Joseph Gillet, but here we need only consider the Spanish ones before 1559. The first appears to be an edition printed by Cromberger and almost certainly of Seville, 1526, which survives in a single mutilated copy; it contains the two missing plays, presumably written in the years 1517–20. Others followed: Seville, 1533–4, 1545, and a later one which will be discussed in its place further on.

Three separate editions of single plays by Torres printed in Spain were recorded by Joseph Gillet:

Comedia Tinellaria, Toledo, Ramón de Petras, 1524. The title-page includes six figurines and two wood-blocks of houses. 4°. a–b^8 (G. 17).

Comedia Jacinta, [?Burgos, Juan de Junta (1535–40)]. 4°. a^{12} (G. 16).

Comedia Aquilana, Burgos, Juan de Junta, 1552. Title-page with wood-block of St John the Evangelist on an eagle. 4°. A–C^{8} (G. 19).

From Torres Naharro later dramatists copied the division of a play into acts, not necessarily into five acts. The 'introit' and the statement of the argument were also imitated, though many later writers dispensed with them.

Mr Norton fixed his self-imposed chronological limit at 31 December, 1520. After that date we must rely largely on facsimiles of dramas produced chiefly by the Royal Spanish Academy[6] and on regional bibliographies, mostly of the late nineteenth century. Not all these books are equally accurate, but at least they give us details about title-pages and formats which we cannot find elsewhere. Sometimes we can check them by comparing their statements with modern critical editions, a very few specialised monographs and single copies in British libraries. Our chief lack in this part of our account is of typographical identifications of works issued without date or imprint; we can only hope that some other competent scholar will follow Mr Norton in the methodical study of Spanish book-production after 1520.

All the collected editions of plays printed before 1521 in Spain had been folios (Encina, 1496 and later editions; Lucas Fernández, 1514; Urrea, 1513 and 1516; Torres Naharro, 1520) except for the large singly-quired quarto by Alfonso de Castrillo of 1520. A change set in some time later, for the *Propalladia* of Seville, 1533–4 is a quarto (a^{4} b–p^{8} q^{10} ^{2}a^{20} – the last gathering contains the *Comedia Aquilana*), and so is that of Seville, 1545 (a–e^{8} f^{4} g–p^{8} q^{10} ^{2}a^{20} – with the last gathering as in the earlier Seville edition). Perhaps the only other important collection of plays and poems by a single author during these years – Diego Sánchez de Badajoz's *Recopilacion en metro* (A–M^{8} N^{4} O–V^{8} X^{4})

[6] *Autos, comedias y farsas de la Biblioteca Nacional*, two volumes with a preface by Justo García Morales, Madrid, 1962.

– appeared also as a quarto at Seville in 1554.[7] Henceforward the usual format for printed Spanish plays – both *sueltas* and in collections – was the quarto. Some octavos also are to be found; but were there (except for the two editions of Gil Vicente's *Copilaçam de todas las obras* of 1562 and 1586) any folio prints of them after 1550? Gil Vicente wrote most of his plays in Portuguese, and they were printed by his son Luis and his daughter Paula in Lisbon.[8]

An examination of the format of *comedias sueltas* before 1560 yields no firm conclusions about printers' preferences for one fat or several moderately slender gatherings. The three *Terno* plays by Vasco Díaz Tanco de Fregenal have title-pages and are in three separate quarto gatherings; according to Sánchez they were printed at Saragossa during the years 1528–30. Earlier but also from Saragossa were Jaime de Güete's *Comedia llamada Vidriana*, with title-page, but not imprint or date; it collates a^8 b^{10}. His *Comedia llamada Tesorina*[9] has similar characteristics but collates a–b^8. Two editions of Hernán López de Yanguas's *Farsa del mundo*, with dated title-pages of 1524 and 1528, collate a–b^8 also. The *Tragicomedia alegorica del parayso y del infierno*, Burgos, Juan de Junta, and with a title-page dated 1539, consists of a single twelve-leaf quarto gathering. So does the anonymous *Farsa llamada Rosiela*, Cuenca, 1558. Luis de Miranda's well-written *Comedia prodiga*, printed at Seville by Martín de Montesdoca in 1554, has a title-page and the collation of a–b^{12}; the equally moving *Tragedia llamada Josefina* by Micael de Carvajal, printed by Juan de

[7] Also available in a Royal Spanish Academy facsimile of 1929. There is a good modern text by Frida Weber de Kurlat, University of Buenos Aires, 1968.

[8] See the facsimile edition of the 1562 *Copilaçam de todalas obras de Gil Vicente*, Lisbon, 1928, fols. ꝗii^r and iii^v.

[9] Juan M. Sánchez, *Bibliografia aragonesa del siglo XVI*, 2 vols., Madrid, 1913–14, nos. 172–4, 151–2.

Ayala of Toledo,[10] has a title-page and collates a–d.[8] These are scattered examples; possibly a more complete survey might establish whether or not plays in a single gathering of eight, ten or twelve leaves and with head-titles catered for a less wealthy public than did those with more elaborate collations which appealed to the better educated, more prosperous classes. From about 1520 onwards we find from time to time on title-pages and in head-titles the use of wood-block figurines to represent the different characters in the play in question.

The inquisitional *Index* of 1559 was the first Spanish attempt to cover works of humane letters as well as those of theology.[11] It listed the following dramatic items:

Acaescimiento, o comedia llamada Orphea, dirigida al muy Illustre y assi magnifico señor don Pedro de Arellano conde de Aguilar.

Auto hecho nueuamente por Gil Vice[n]te, sobre los muy altos y muy dulces amores de Amadis de Gaula con la Princesa Oriana hija del Rey Lisuarte.

Comedia llamada Iacinta, compuesta & impressa, con vna epistola familiar.

Comedia llamada Aquilana, hecha por Bartholome de Torres Naharro.

Comedia llamada Thesorina, hecha nueuamente por Iayme de Huete.

[10] With one exception (the *Tragedia Josefina*) these plays are to be found in the volumes referred to in note 6 above. See nos. III, XVI, XV, V, VI, X, XXIV, XXI. The *Josefina* was edited by Gillet, Princeton, 1932. There were other early editions of this interesting play.

[11] The earliest edition of this *Index* was dated 2 September, 1559; the other copies we have seen are later but keep the date of the year only. *Cathalogus librorũ, qui prohibẽtur mãdato Illustrissimi & Reuerend. D. D. Ferdinandi de Valdes Hispaleñ. Archiep̃i, Inquisitoris Generalis Hispaniæ*, Pinciae [= Valladolid], 1559. We have used the Royal Spanish Academy's facsimile in *Tres índices expurgatorios de la Inquisición española en el siglo XVI*, Madrid, 1952. This reprint contains items added a few years after the above-mentioned first edition.

Comedia llamada Tidea, compuesta por Francisco de las Natas. (p. 39)

Egloga nueuamente trobada por Iua[n] del Enzina: en la qual se introduzen dos enamorados, llamados Placido [sic] y Victoriano. (p. 40)

Farsa llamada Custodia.

Farsa llamada Iosephina.

Farsa de dos enamorados. (p. 41)

Propaladia, hecha por Bartholome de Torres Naharro. (p. 47)

One may doubt whether any of the dramatic works proscribed in 1559 was deliberately heretical in intention, though the discovery of fragments of the *Josefina*, in Spanish but printed in Hebrew characters (perhaps by Soncino), must be taken into account.[12] (The case of the reprinting in Amsterdam in 1726 of Calderón's *Judas Macabeo* and *Los cabellos de Absalón* – admittedly a much later parallel – can be attributed to the wish of the Dutch Sephardim to read a dramatic version in Spanish of Old Testament subjects.) Two of the rules for expurgation, printed in some seventeenth-century indexes, give us at least a hint of the inquisitional objections. Rule VII begins:

> Books that treat of, relate and teach things purposely lascivious, either of love or of other matters, are prohibited as hurtful to the virtuous customs of the Christian Church, even if heresies and errors in faith are not mingled in them, so we order that those which contain them be severely castigated by the inquisitors. [*Or perhaps*: those who own them be severely punished by the inquisitors.][13]

[12] J. L. Teicher, 'Hebrew printed fragments', *The Bodleian Library Record*, I, xiv (1941), 234–6.

[13] Prohibense assimismo los libros que tratan, cuentan, y enseñan cosas de proposito lascivas, de amores, o otras qualesquiera, como dañosas a las buenas costumbres de la Yglesia Christiana, aunque no se mezclen en ellos heregias, y errores en la Fè, mandando que los que los tuvieren sean castigados por los Inquisidores severamente: edition of Madrid, 1667, p. ix, col. b.

And in Rule XVI we find:

> Words from Holy Scripture applied impiously for profane purposes shall be expurgated . . .
>
> Phrases that attack the good reputation of neighbours and specially those that contain reflections on ecclesiastics and princes and those that are opposed to virtuous customs and Christian discipline must be cancelled . . .
>
> Also jokes and witticisms published to the offense or detriment of neighbours [must be cancelled] . . . Also lascivious writings that can damage virtuous customs . . .[14]

The rigorous application of those two rules could and did lead to the ban imposed on eloquent love-scenes, on the use of words like *divino* applied to human beings, on oaths phrased in religious terms, on parodies of Biblical phrases, on even mild suspicions of anti-clericalism and on anything that seemed to the inquisitors to encourage sins of the flesh. The results of these strictures can be seen in Gillet's examination of the purged *Propalladia*, printed in Madrid fourteen years later than that Draconian *Index*. He showed how oaths like *Voto a Dios* became *O gran Dios* or other euphemisms, how in the *Comedia Soldadesca* the friar without a religious vocation, who strips off his habit before he enlists in the army, is shown as merely a willing civilian recruit, how all the references to adoration of women by their lovers were carefully removed. There can be little doubt that the decrees of 1559 must have come as a severe shock to playwrights, to actors and to printers, to say nothing of the theatre-going public. A considerable number of plays had been condemned, and the reasons that underlay that

[14] Devense expurgar qualesquier palabras de la sagrada Escritura aplicadas impiamente para usos profanos . . . Hanse de borrar las clausulas detractorias de la buena fama de los proximos, y principalmente las que contienen detraccion de Eclesiasticos, y Principes, y las que se oponen a las buenas costumbres, y a la disciplina Christiana . . . Tambien los chistes y gracias publicadas en ofensa, o perjuizio, y buen credito de los proximos . . . Item los Escritos lascivos que pueden viciar las buenas costumbres: *ed. cit.*, p. xiv.

verdict applied also to many others whose names were not recorded. Here, perhaps, is the reason why Diego Sánchez de Badajoz's *Recopilación en metro* survives only in an unique copy; even though his works were robustly pious, he was not averse to pointing out (e.g. in his *Farsa militar*) how a religious could fall a victim to the world, the flesh and the devil.

The years between 1559 and the end of the century have been little studied from our point of view. Spanish compilers of facsimiles tend to prefer works printed in black-letter types to those in roman; and in an earlier chapter we noted how roman types did not become predominant until the latter part of the sixteenth century. Sánchez noted that Bartolomé Palau's *Victoria Christi* appeared as a quarto printed by Miguel de Güessa of Saragossa in 1589; la Barrera tells us that three plays by Alonso de la Vega appeared as *sueltas* between 1560 and 1563. Despite the fact that Philip II established Madrid as the capital of Castile in 1561, and the opening of permanent theatres in that city in the 1570s, few plays were printed there before 1601. Though Madrid soon became the real centre of Spanish theatrical life and – partly because of the growth of this new capital, partly because of the genius of Lope de Vega – soon dominated the regions, yet the provinces continued to produce dramatic collections until well into the seventeenth century. Translations of Terence were printed at Saragossa in 1577, to be reprinted at Alcalá in 1583 and at Barcelona in 1599. Timoneda printed his own *Tres comedias* as an octavo in 1559 at Valencia, plays probably by other Valencians in his *Turiana* in 1563–5, and his two sets called *Ternario sacramental* in the same city in 1575. Earlier he had printed Lope de Rueda's italianate prose *comedias* and *pasos* (one-act farces) also in Valencia and as an octavo in 1567, to be reprinted at Seville in 1576 and at Logroño in 1588. Juan de la Cueva's *Primera parte de las comedias y tragedias* appeared at Seville in 1588. Of these works Timoneda's *Turiana* represented an innovation in the printing of Spanish plays which seems to us to deserve separate treatment in a new paragraph.

The *Turiana* is a quarto. The apparently unique surviving copy is imperfect. The existence of a Spanish Academy reprint in facsimile (1936) makes a detailed collation unnecessary. There are two unsigned preliminary leaves which contain a licence from the Valencian Inquisition on the verso of the title-page, dated 26 April 1563, an undated privilege for four years from the Governor and Captain-general of Valencia on the recto of the second leaf and a dedication to the same gentleman on its verso. The first gathering of the text is signed B[i]-v and consists of eight leaves. It contains five *passos* or farces which have a final colophon on B8^v:

> Vidit Michael Carrança Prouincialis Carmelita. Theologus & corrector S. Inquisitionis Valeñ. 26. Apri. 1564 [sic]. ¶ Con priuilegio Real por quatro años. Año. M.D.lxiiij.

Gathering C – which originally had twelve leaves, of which seven are signed – contains the *Tragi comedia llamada Filomena*. It begins with a title-page of its own which contains ten figurines to represent the ten persons of the drama; each is given the title of the appropriate character. At the foot of the title-page are the words:

> [leaf ornament] Impressa en Valencia en casa de Ioan Mey. 1564. Con licencia del sancto officio. Y priuilegio Real.

The plays ends on C11^v, but the original presence of a twelfth leaf is betrayed by the final catchword *Glosa*, which is obviously the first word of the title of a lost poem added at the end of the play to complete the gathering. The following play, the *Farça llamada Paliana*, occupies gathering D^{10}; it too has ten figurines appropriately labelled on the title-page, along with the date 1564. The colophon reads:

> [leaf ornament] Fue impressa la presente obra en la muy noble y coronada ciudad de Valencia en casa de Ioan Mey. 1564

On the last page there is a fill-up poem in Valencian Catalan entitled *Canço*. The *Comedia llamada Aurelia* fills all but the last page of gathering E of twelve leaves. Its title-page and imprint are similar to those already described. There is no colophon.

On the last page there is a *Cancion* in Castilian and a final ornament similar to that at the end of gathering D. The print is dated 1564. There is no trace of a gathering F, and the signatures of gathering G indicate the omission of the second leaf of the *Farça llamada Trapaçera.* The penultimate leaf also is missing, and the final one contains eleven ten-line stanzas printed in roman type (all the rest of the text is in black-letter); they clearly do not belong to the play. The colophon, if there ever was one, is missing, but the title-page is dated 1565. The *Farça llamada Rosalina* occupies the ten leaves of gathering H; its title-page is dated 1565 too, and there is no colophon, but on the last page we find the final ornament already encountered on leaves D10^{v} and E12^{v}. Of the *Farça llamada Floriana* we have only the two outer leaves, the last of which has the same final ornament. We cannot estimate how many inner leaves have been lost.

The *Paliana* is undivided, as are the *Trapaçera* and the *Rosalina*; the *Filomena* is divided into seven scenes and the *Aurelia* into five *jornadas.* The preliminaries to the book and the title-pages of the separate items it contains are in roman, but all the texts are in black letter. We cannot tell how much, how many plays are missing at the end of this interesting but fragmentary volume. There can, however, be no doubt that its make-up was conceived in order that the whole could be sold either as a complete volume or as separate *sueltas.* Had the project been merely to get rid of a lot of *sueltas* already in stock with two preliminary leaves at the front they would not have been signed A, B, C, D, F, G and H. Each separate play would have begun with a gathering signed A. If the book had been designed exclusively to be sold entire there would have been no reason to advertise in imprints and in colophons the fact that each play in it had ecclesiastical approval and to name the printer and the dates of issue (this is the principal difference between this volume and the *Farsas y eglogas* of Lucas Fernández). We shall find comparable volumes printed in the next century, but the circumstances of their issue almost certainly varied.

During these years in Madrid the purged edition of Torres Naharro's *Propalladia* came out in 1573. We must regret the expurgations to which Juan López de Velasco subjected it, but a purged *Propalladia* was better than no *Propalladia* at all. Gillet's examination of the book can hardly be bettered (G. 9).[15] It must have influenced the young Lope de Vega, whose first drafts may date from the eighties. The only other significant dramatic works printed in the capital before 1601 appeared as a volume with the title *Primeras tragedias españolas* by Jerónimo Bermúdez (alias Antonio de Silva) in 1577. The two tragedies were entitled *Nise lastimosa* and *Nise laureada*, the first adapted from a Portuguese tragedy by Antonio Ferreira, the second Bermúdez's own work. These plays probably helped on the neoclassical theatrical genre which affected Captain Virués in Valencia, Lupercio Leonardo de Argensola in Saragossa and perhaps also Juan de la Cueva in Seville. Bermúdez's book was an octavo.[16]

In the early years of the seventeenth century we can find survivals of the *suelta* printed in the form of one or two more or less bulky gatherings. In 1603 in Medina del Campo Juan Godínez (or Gudínez) de Millis printed Andrés Prado's *Farsa . . . llamada Cornelia* (quarto, A^4, with a head title and five figurines), Juan de Rodrigo Alonso's *Comedia [de] la Sancta Susana* (quarto, A^8), and Diego Sánchez de Badajoz's *Farsa sobre el matrimonio* (quarto, A^8).[17] Cristóbal Pérez Pastor reprinted a *Danza del Santissimo Nacimiento de nuestro Señor Iesu Christo, al modo pastoril*, with a title-page and wood-block

[15] Gillet, *Propalladia*, i, 55–71, especially 64–71.

[16] C. Pérez Pastor, *Bibliografía madrileña*, 3 vols., Madrid, 1891–1917; i, item 117.

[17] C. Pérez Pastor, *La imprenta en Medina del Campo*, Madrid, 1895, items 262–4. *Autos y farsas de la Biblioteca Nacional* reproduces *Cornelia* (XXVII), the 1558 Alcalá edition of *Susanna* (IX: 4°, A^8. Juan de Rodrigo Alonso is also known as Juan de Pedraza), and the *Farsa sobre el matrimonio* (VIII). In the last, the editors accept the absurd 1530 of the head-title, not the 1603 of the colophon.

of the Nativity in four unsigned quarto leaves, composed by Pedro Suárez de Robles and printed by Miguel Serrano de Vargas, Madrid, 1606. (This play was written for performance in church.)[18] Joaquín Montaner recorded from the library of Arturo Sedó (now in that of the Instituto del Teatro at Barcelona) three *sueltas* by Gaspar de Aguilar (one is really by Guillén de Castro) and one by Canon Tárrega, which appeared in a composite volume published in Valencia in 1608 (we shall examine it a little later) and two others by the latter to be dated for similar reasons in that volume's second part of 1616.[19]

Before then the *comedia* proper had already taken shape. In the latter part of the reign of Philip II Torres Naharro's five acts were gradually reduced from four to three. Though Captain Virués (1550–1610?) divided his *Elisa Dido – tragedia conforme al arte antiguo* – into five acts, his four other surviving tragedies are in three. Juan de la Cueva's plays are in four acts, as is Micer Andrés Rey de Artieda's *Los amantes* (printed in Valencia in 1581). Cervantes's two early tragedies *El trato de Argel* and *La Numancia* (which were not printed until 1784) were in four acts, but the eight *comedias,* printed in Madrid in 1615, were all in three. Torres's 'introit' had by then been transformed into an introductory prologue (*loa*) and soon lost any possible connection with the play that followed it. Equally irrelevant (but sometimes very funny) one-act farces (*entremeses*) and spoken or sung ballets called *bailes* were performed between the acts or at the end of the play. (These were nearly always printed separately, not together with the plays they interrupted.) Lope's early plays patterned the new form of the *comedia* itself, which dealt largely, but not exclusively, with problems of love and honour, of mistakes in identity, and with

[18] Pérez Pastor, *Bibliografia madrileña*, ii (1906), item 951.

[19] J. Montaner, *La colección teatral de don Arturo Sedó*, Barcelona, 1951, pp.33–4, 63–4.

an anti-hero called the *gracioso* (clown). The prevailing form was comedy, but tragedy was sometimes just around the corner, and occasionally (if one considers the large number of Spanish plays at this period) tragedy was obviously dominant. Lope's great lyrical gifts, his dramatic sense and his ability to collaborate with the professional actors and to please a wide public enabled the new *genre* to conquer the Madrid and provincial stages, almost without a struggle.[20]

In 1603 Pedro Craesbeeck printed in Lisbon six plays attributed to Lope, of which only two were his. This was an octavo. The following year a volume of twelve plays by him, a quarto, came out in Valencia. The title read *Las comedias del famoso poeta Lope de Vega Carpio*, but it is usually referred to as the '*Primera parte de las comedias de Lope*'. It was reprinted in Valladolid (and perhaps in Madrid) in the same year and later on in other cities inside and outside Spain; there were in all fourteen editions of this book before 1627, including those of Lisbon, Antwerp, Brussels and Saragossa. Its success encouraged the issue of further editions in the following years: *Segunda parte* (Madrid, Alonso Martín) 1609; *Tercera parte* ('Barcelona, Sebastián de Cormellas', but really by Gabriel Ramos Vejarano of Seville: see our Chapter II) 1612; *Quarta parte* (Madrid, Miguel Serrano de Vargas) 1614, and a *Quinta parte* (Alcalá de Henares, widow of Luis Martínez) 1615; both the *Tercera parte* and the *Quinta parte* were *desglosables*, and of the latter we are told that each play was separately paged – i.e. the volume was really made up of twelve *sueltas*. Other editions with different plays in them await further investigation. Nine more *partes de Lope* were printed by 1620. Each of these *partes* con-

[20] N. D. Shergold, *A history of the Spanish stage from medieval times until the end of the seventeenth century*, Oxford, 1967, chapters 7 and 8; E. M. Wilson and D. Moir, *A literary history of Spain – The Golden Age drama (1492–1700)*, London and New York, 1971, chapter 3.

tained twelve plays; all were quartos.[21] The *partes* of later dramatists usually kept to this pattern, as did the irregular set of the *partes de diferentes o de varios* (?1632–?53) and the forty-eight volumes known as the *comedias escogidas* (1652–1704). These works have often been criticised for their textual defects, but we often have to make do with them for lack of better texts. Usually they were produced without the permission of, or any correction by, the original authors. Lope apparently had some say in the preparation of his fourth, seventh, eighth and ninth *partes* and in many of the later ones.[22]

The success of the so-called *Primera parte* of Lope perhaps encouraged the Valencian printers to look nearer home in order to produce two other quarto volumes of plays by the interesting, if minor, group of dramatists from that city. The first was printed in 1608 (apparently one or two copies have the date 1609) with the title: *Doze comedias famosas de quatro poetas naturales de la insigne y coronada ciudad de Valencia*. These plays were collected by Aurelio Mey, presumably a relative of (?Juan) Felipe Mey and of Pedro Patricio Mey, printers in that city. We doubt whether Aurelio Mey was really the printer of the preliminaries to this book; they consist of four leaves, which contain a licence in Valencian Catalan from the Marqués de Caracena dated 30 August 1608, two *aprobaciones* dated

[21] H. A. Rennert, 'Bibliography of the dramatic works of Lope de Vega', *Revue Hispanique*, xxxiii (1915), 1–284. See also A. Castro and Rennert, *Vida de Lope de Vega (1562–1635)*, notas adicionales de Fernando Lázaro Carreter, Salamanca, 1969, pp. 157–8, 176, 199–200, 207–8, 216–17, 240–2, 433–5; and Maria G. Profeti, 'Appunti bibliografici sulla collezione "Diferentes autores"', *Miscellanea di studi ispanici*, Pisa, 1969–70, 123–86, especially 129–35. For the *Tercera parte*, see Luis Vélez de Guevara, *Los hijos de la barbuda*, ed. M. G. Profeti, Pisa, 1970, p. 10; and J. Moll, 'La "Tercera parte de las comedias de Lope de Vega y otros autores", falsificación sevillana', *Revista de Archivos, Bibliotecas y Museos*, lxxvii (1974), 625, n. 23.

[22] See for example Castro and Rennert, *Vida de Lope de Vega*, pp. 207–8, 230, 240–2; but also A. González Palencia, 'Pleito entre Lope de Vega y un editor de sus comedias', *Boletín de la Biblioteca Menéndez Pelayo*, iii (1921), 17–26.

29 and 30 August, a dedicatory poem to the Marqués from Aurelio Mey and a list of the plays and authors included in the volume, which does not coincide in its order with that in the copy we have examined.[23] The plays are well and spaciously printed; many have amusing wood-block figurines either on the title-page or in some other suitable place in the *suelta*. (Three title-pages are reproduced in the edition of Valencian dramatists edited by Eduardo Juliá Martínez.[24]) Blank pages occur from time to time too: each *suelta* and the volume as a whole were designed to impress the intending purchaser. The authors represented were Canon Tárrega (six plays), Gaspar Aguilar (three plays), Guillén de Castro (two plays) and Miguel Beneyto (one play). *Loas* were printed for eight plays, with two in Tárrega's *El prado de Valencia*; an *entremés* is printed after Beneyto's *El hiio obediente*; poems were added to fill the last gathering by Guillén de Castro after his *El amor constante* and by Aguilar after his *La nuera humilde*. The volume, in view of its great rarity and interest, deserves a fuller description than can be given here. We shall confine ourselves to giving the collations of each item in it and to the discussion of the signatures themselves. The six plays by Tárrega collate as follows: 1. *El cerco de Rodas*, A–B^{8} C^{4}; 2. *Las suertes trocadas y torneo venturoso*, A–C^{8} D^{10}; 3. *La perseguida Amaltea*, A–B^{8} C^{6}; 4. *El prado de Valencia*, A–C^{8} D^{4}; 5. *El fingido esposo*, A–B^{8} C^{4}; 6. *La sangre leal de los montañeses de Navarra*, A–B^{8} C^{6}. Those by Aguilar: 7. *Los amantes de Cartago*, A–B^{8} C^{4}; 8. *La nuera humilde*, A–C^{8}; 9. *La gitana melancolica*, A–C^{8}. Those by Castro: 10. *El cavallero bovo*, A–B^{8} C^{4}; 11. *El amor constante*, A–C^{8} D^{4}. That by Beneyto: 12. *El hiio obediente*, A–C^{8}. The two last-mentioned plays by Tárrega (nos. 5 and 6) according to their colophons were printed in 1608 by Pedro Patricio Mey. We also note that the signatures are numbered according to the Roman system in

[23] Clare College, Cambridge: Fellows' Library, W.7. 14.

[24] *Poetas dramáticos valencianos,* 2 vols., Madrid, 1929; i, pp. XCV, CXIII, CXXVII. The title-page of the complete volume is illustrated on p. LVIII.

our nos. 1, 2, 3, 4, 8, 9, 11 and 12; the others are in Arabic numbers. The *sueltas* with Arabic numerals also have different type; they perhaps were the work of the printer of nos. 5 and 6: Pedro Patricio Mey. The book is therefore not homogeneous in its printing. But it compares most favourably – as far as readability and spacing are concerned – with the contents of Pepys 1553 and with later *sueltas* printed in Seville by the Leefdaels and the Padrinos.[25]

The *Doze comedias* were reprinted in 1609 in Barcelona by Sebastián de Cormellas and in 1614 in Madrid by Miguel Serrano de Vargas. We have not seen the Barcelona edition, but the printers of the Madrid one tried, at least initially, to produce *desglosables*. There is no pagination, and although signatures are continuous, the first four plays are divided as follows: *El prado de Valencia*, A–C^{8} D^{4}; *El esposo fingido*, E–F^{8} G^{4}; *El cerco de Rodas*, H–I^{8} K^{4}; and *La perseguida Amaltea*, L–N^{8}. The volume then collates O–Ss^{8} Tt^{4}, and plays (or the poems accompanying them) run from one gathering into the next (B.L. copy, 11725. cc. 10). That this was no positive drawback to disbinding is shown by the existence of a copy of *La gitana melancolica*, the seventh play, in a volume of *sueltas* and disbound fragments (B.L., T. 1737[22]).[26] A second part, with a new title, was published at Valencia in 1616, edited again by Aurelio Mey and printed by Felipe Mey. It was entitled: *Norte de la poesia española. Illustrado del sol de doze Comedias (que forman Segunda parte) de Laureados Poetas Valencianos: y de doze escogidas Loas, y otras Rimas a varios sugetos.* The dramatists

[25] The best description of this book which we have seen is that in P. Salvá y Mallén, *Catálogo de la biblioteca de Salvá*, 2 vols., Valencia, 1872, i, item 1357.

[26] *La gitana* occupies the last four leaves of X and Y–Aa^{8}, twenty-eight leaves; the sewing is not clearly visible in the T.1737 copy. Leaf A1 of volume 11725.cc.10 is not conjugate with A8; the original A1 has been removed and the new one (containing the *loa*) is conjugate with a new title-leaf (with the date 1614, but really *c.* 1680?). This gives five preliminary leaves, for the original four are still present. See also Salvá, *Catálogo,* items 1358–9.

included Tárrega: *El cerco de Pavia y prision del Rey de Francia*; *La duquesa constante*; *La fundacion de la Orden de la Merced* (with collations in that order: A–C^8 D^4; A–C^8; A–B^8 C^{10}). Aguilar: *El mercader amante*; *La fuerza del interes*; *La suerte sin esperanza*; *El gran patriarcha don Iuan de Ribera* (collations: A–B^8 C^6; A–C^8; A–B^8 C^6; A–C^8). 'Ricardo de Turia' (? = Pedro Juan de Rejaule y Toledo): *La burladora burlada*; *La belligera española*; *La fe pagada*; *El triumfante martirio y gloriosa muerte de San Vicente* (collations: A–B^8 C^{10}; A–B^8 C^{12}; A–B^8 C^{12}; A–B^8 C^{10}). Carlos Boil: *El marido asigurado* (collation: A–B^8 C^{12}).[27]

As far as we can tell this second part was never reprinted. The Valencians had not shot their last bolt with the two works referred to in the last two paragraphs. Their most famous playwright, Guillén de Castro (b. Valencia, 1569; d. Madrid, 1631), whose play about the Cid was adapted to the rules of neoclassical drama by Pierre Corneille, published his *Primera parte* in Valencia in 1618, his *Segunda parte* in the same city in 1625. A variant issue of the *Primera parte* appeared in 1621; only the first two leaves – the preliminaries – were new. They included an *aprobación* by Don Juan de Jáuregui, dated Madrid, 20 April 1621, and Castro's new dedication to Lope de Vega's daughter Marcela. The imprints of both title-pages name Felipe Mey as the printer of the book, but the second issue's preliminaries must have been printed in Madrid.[28] We have seen the second issue in the Lilly Library at Bloomington, Indiana. The *sueltas* in it are less remarkable than those of the *Doze comedias* of 1609, but the compartments and the figurines

[27] Juliá Martínez, *Poetas dramáticos valencianos*; reproductions of the title-pages of *sueltas* are shown on pp. LXXXII, CIX, CXIX and CXXII of the first volume. See also Salvá, *Catálogo*, item 1360. We produce this description by combining information from Salvá and the B.L. copy (also 11725.cc.10); this copy lacks leaf C8 of Aguilar's *El gran patriarcha*, almost certainly blank, and all of the last play, *El triumfante martirio . . . de San Vicente*. Salvá does not give a collation for *El gran patriarcha*. The B.L. has another copy of *El marido asigurado* bound in T.1737(25).

[28] Edited in three volumes by Eduardo Juliá Martínez, Madrid, 1925–7. He first discovered the nature of the 1621 issue: i, XXIV–XXIX.

on the title-pages show still an attempt to please their readers' eyes. Juliá Martínez reproduced the two title-pages, as well as those of the three plays that have Cervantine sources (*Don Quixote de la Mancha*, *El curioso impertinente* and *La fuerza de la sangre*) in his edition of Castro's plays of 1925–7. The collations of the twelve separate plays show similar make-up to those we have already quoted: four plays collate A–B^{8} C^{10}; five A–C^{8}; two A–B^{8} C^{6} and one A^{8} B^{12}. We have not seen his *Segunda parte*. The reproduction of the title-page of *La fuerza de la sangre* shows the signature Ii at the foot of the page; the volume cannot be made up of *sueltas*.[29] The same reproduction shows one head ornament but no compartments or figurines. Felipe Mey of Valencia had begun to follow the fashions of Madrid.

The extensive sales of Lope's *partes* – as often as not unauthorised and with corrupt texts – are partly a cause and partly a symptom of the general lowering of printing standards. Printers found that they had to cut their costs as far as they could, so they used as cheap paper as they could buy. They began to crowd their pages by making necessary spaces as small as possible. They would begin a new play in the middle of a page whose top was occupied by the last lines of the one that went before it. Act divisions would occur in only one column instead of crossing a two-columned page. Dated *sueltas* became rare and so did title-pages. Figurines occurred only occasionally below the head-titles, wood-block ornaments appeared only to fill up space left at the end of a given play. Legibility was often obscured by bad inking and damaged types. All these defects were perhaps to be expected among provincial printers who were often engaged in unauthorised reprints and piracies. Only occasionally were there printed *sueltas* that had some distinction in their printing; these were nearly always circulated

[29] The various title-pages mentioned are reproduced in Juliá's edition: i, XXV, XXVII; ii, XIII, XIX, XXIII; iii, XXI. Salvá, *Catálogo*, item 1154, also records continuous pagination (up to 556) in the *Segunda parte*.

privately or for a special purpose. A few notes on some of them follow.

(a) D. Antonio [Hurtado] de Mendoza, *Querer por solo querer,* Madrid, Juan de la Cuesta, 1623. This is an edition of a play written to celebrate Queen Isabel de Borbón's birthday, acted by the ladies (*meninas*) of the Court and dedicated to Her Majesty. The title-page contains the royal arms, and Don Antonio's dedication follows on the second leaf. His apology follows: he is printing this play solely for the benefit of those who ask for it.[30] A list of the persons in the drama follows: it gives the names of all the aristocratic actresses. The *loa* comes next, occupying two leaves, and after a blank leaf the first act begins. It collates: gr^4 ggr^2 A–E^8[F]^2 – gathering F is signed E by mistake. The preliminaries (and of course the blank leaf) are unfoliated [i–vi], the text of the play itself is foliated: 1–42. The verso of the title-page and the last page are blank. The play is – for its time – well printed.[31]

(b) Frey Lope Félix de Vega Carpio, *El castigo sin venganza, tragedia*, Barcelona, Pedro Lacavallería, 1634. There can be no doubt that Lope himself commissioned this print; one suspects that it was paid for by the Duke of Sessa. Its preliminaries contain an *aprobación* by a Barcelona Dominican, dated 23 July 1634, Lope's dedication to his patron the Duke, and in a short but meaty prologue he tells his readers that they can take it for his own work, because it was not printed in Seville (where covetous book-sellers have no scruples about altering the names of authors and no regard for the reputations of other men). He also warned them that he has not followed classical

[30] Esta Comedia no la consiento yo impressa; sufrola assi trasladada, para repartirla entre los que la piden, que no tengo presuncion de ofrecersela à nadie. gr2^v [Professor Wilson's copy, now in the University Library, Cambridge – D.W.C.]

[31] R. M. Flores, *The compositors of the first and second Madrid editions of Don Quixote Part I*, London, 1975, Appendix I, item 89.

precepts but written a tragedy in Spanish style.[32] It consists of only one gathering – A^{28} – with the last leaf missing in the facsimile, probably blank, and leaves 2–14 are signed. The twenty-seven surviving leaves are unnumbered. The original manuscript was edited by J. A. van Dam in 1928, who compared his source with this edition and decided that the text of the *suelta* was reasonably good, and that in it there are a few variants that may be attributed to the poet rather than to the printer.[33] This is one of Lope's finest plays, and we can be grateful that he sent the manuscript to the printer. There is only one complete copy of this *suelta* known to scholars; it is in the Madrid Biblioteca Nacional.[34] It is a reasonable example of provincial seventeenth-century printing. The play was also printed posthumously in the *Parte XXI* of Madrid, 1635, and in *Doze comedias las mas grandiosas . . .*, Lisbon, 1647.

(c) Anonymous, *La famosa comedia de la entrada del Marques de los Velez en Cathaluña, Rota de las tropas castellanas, y assalto de Moniuich* [sic], Barcelona, Jayme Romeu, 1641. This was a work of anti-Castilian, pro-Catalan propaganda during the Civil War of 1640–52. There are some lines in it in Catalan, but most of the play is written in Castilian (including the apparition of St Eulalia to Pau Claris). It has a title-page on which there are two figurines (the verso is blank) and a pro-

[32] Señor Lector, esta Tragedia se hizo en la Corte solo vn dia, por causas que a v.m. le importan poco. Dexò entonces tantos deseosos de verla, que los he querido satisfazer con imprimirla . . . V.m. la lea por mia, porque no es impressa en Seuilla, cuyos Libreros, atendiendo a la ganancia, baraja[n] los nombres de los Poetas, y a vnos dan sietes, y a otros sotas, que ay hombres, que por dinero no reparan en el honor ageno, que a bueltas de sus mal impressos libros venden, y compran. Aduirtiendo que està escrita al estilo Español, no por la antiguedad Griega, y seueridad Latina, huyendo de las sombras, Nuncios, y coros; porque el gusto puede mudar los preceptos, como el vso los trages, y el tiempo las costumbres. $A3^{v}$.

[33] *El castigo sin venganza* . . . [edited by] C. F. A. van Dam, Groningen, Madrid and Paris, 1928, p. 11.

[34] We have used the facsimile edition with a final note by Miguel Artigas printed in Lope's *La Circe con otras Rimas y Prosas*, Madrid, 1935 (Colección Tesoro).

logue on the second leaf which ends with two stanzas (*décimas*) in Catalan from the works of Don Benito García, Rector of Vallfogona. The play has little literary merit, but it exhibits the feelings of the Catalans after the failure of the Castilian army to storm Barcelona. Although the second leaf is signed ꝯ2, the first lines of the text begin on leaf A3. It seems to collate (we are using an imperfect copy) A–C8 D4, foliated [ii]+26 leaves. There were other editions: Salvá and Montaner mention one of 1642, and there is an undated copy in the British Library (absurdly attributed in the Catalogue to ?Madrid, ?1700). Apparently in some copies there were printed a *loa* and an *entremés* of Catalan farmers and Castilian soldiers, but these we have not seen. The paper is poor and the printing crude.[35]

(d) [Don Pedro Calderón de la Barca], *Fieras afemina amor*, n.i., n.d. [but probably Madrid, Julián de Paredes, 1670]. This play was lavishly produced in January 1670, though the performance had originally been planned for 22 December 1669. The occasion was the birthday of the Queen-Mother, Mariana of Austria, Philip IV's widow and mother of Charles II, then a small boy of six. The paper on which it is printed is excellent and the typography good for its time. It is a quarto with the collation A–Ee4, 112 leaves, foliated. The verso of the title-page and that of the last leaf are blank. It begins with the *loa*, after the first *Jornada* (act) comes an *Entremes Del Triunfo de Iuan Rana* (the celebrated comic actor), after the second a *Segundo sainete de la Fiesta*, and after the third the *Fin de la*

[35] Salvá, *Catálogo*, items 1238–9; Montaner, *La colección teatral de don Arturo Sedó*, pp. 116–17. British Library, C.63.b.34 (1641 edition); 11726.f. 36 (undated edition). [The imperfect copy referred to here was Professor Wilson's, now in the University Library, Cambridge. Before his death he wrote to Dr P. Bohigas in Barcelona, requesting information about copies and editions of this play in libraries there. Dr Bohigas found editions of 1641 and 1642 represented by one copy each in the Sedó and Biblioteca de Cataluña collections, but no copy with a *loa* and *entremés*; one Sedó copy of 1641 could not be traced, however. I thank Dr Bohigas for this information – D.W.C.]

fiesta. The play concerns several of the labours of Hercules and his amorous enslavement by Iole. It is one of the very finest of Calderón's mythological plays, performed in the Buen Retiro Palace. As this *suelta*, obviously designed for those who attended the first performance and perhaps for Mariana's Austrian relatives, could only have been printed from the text of the first performance, we may safely date it 1670. It has already been fully described in English, so we need say no more about it here.[36]

Timoneda had shown the possibility of producing a volume of plays which could be sold either entire or separately as *sueltas*. An example from the early *partes* of Lope shows a more elaborate book. The *Octava parte* of Madrid, 1617, had a straightforward collation: ¶^{4} A–Nn^{8}; the Barcelona reprint of Sebastián de Cormellas so disposed the gatherings that each play formed a unit of its own, which we have indicated by semicolons: ¶^{4} A–B^{8} C^{4}; D–F^{8}; G–I^{8}; K–L^{8} M^{4}; N–O^{8} P^{10}; Q–R^{8} S^{6}; T–V^{8} X^{6}; Y–Z^{8} Aa^{6}; Bb–Cc^{8} Dd^{6}; Ee–Ff^{8} Gg^{6}; Hh–Kk^{8}; Ll–Mm^{8} Nn^{4}; Oo–Pp^{8} Qq^{4}. There were, as usual, twelve plays, but the last unit was a section devoted to minor genres (*entremeses*, *loas*, *bailes*).[37] Some later *partes de varios* and *comedias escogidas* showed the same phenomenon; we give some examples below.

Although the manner of description is not that recommended by Professor Bowers in his *Principles*, Signora Profeti indicates that the following *diferentes/varios* volumes are composed either of *desglosables* or of *sueltas*: *Parte XXVIII*, Huesca, 1634

[36] E. M. Wilson, 'The first edition of Calderón's *Fieras afemina amor*', in *The textual criticism of Calderón's comedias*, pp. 183–200, which is volume i of Pedro Calderón de la Barca, *Comedias* – a facsimile edition prepared by D. W. Cruickshank and J. E. Varey with textual and critical studies, London, 1973. For identification of the printer, see pp. 11–12 of the same volume. [Professor Wilson left an unpublished critical study of this play, and a partially completed critical edition; plans are in hand to publish them – D.W.C.]

[37] There are two copies of the Cormellas edition in Cambridge: University Library, Hisp.7.61.4, and Peterhouse Library, F.10.35.

(pp. 155–7); *Parte XXIX*, Valencia, 1636 (160–1); *Parte XXXI*, Barcelona, 1638 (167–8); *Parte XXXIII*, Valencia, 1642 (171–3) are all *desglosables*, i.e. pagination and/or signatures are continuous, although each play is a bibliographical unit.[38] *Partes XLII*, Saragossa, 1650, *XLIII*, Saragossa, 1650, and *XLIV*, Saragossa, 1652 (175–9), are all volumes of true *sueltas* bound together, as is the curious *Parte XXXXXVII* [sic] misdescribed by her on page 180.

Thanks to the worthy W. R. Chorley some such *desglosadas* have been noted in the British Library copies. We instance two examples by, or partly by, Calderón: *La dama duende*, 11728.h. 15(14) and *El Polifemo*, 11728.h.16(10). The first is foliated 167–91 and signed Aa–Cc^8 with one leaf signed Dd, so it may be incorrect to call it *desglosable*. The second certainly is, for it is foliated 23–42 and collates D–E^8 F^4. Chorley mentions a *Libro de varios*, Lisbon, 1647, i.e. *Doze comedias las mas grandiosas que asta aora han salido, de los mejores y mas insignes poetas, Segunda parte*, Lisbon, Pablo Craesbeeck, 1647 (see under *suelta* (b) above, *El castigo sin venganza*).

As for *Diferentes XLII*, i.e. *Parte quarenta y dos de comedias de diferentes autores*, Saragossa, Juan de Ybar, 1650, we have been able to examine the British Library copy (11725.d.10). It contains four plays by Calderón:

No hay burlas con el amor. Collation: A–B^8 C^6? (only C3 and [C4] are present). Paged 1–?44. The first play in the volume.

El secreto a vozes. Collation: A–C^8. Paged 1–48. The second play in the volume.

[38] Page numbers in this paragraph refer to M. G. Profeti, 'Appunti bibliografici . . .' (see note 21 above). As for *Parte XXXI*, we should point out that our film of the Boston Public Library copy shows that it has not, as Signora Profeti describes, 'segnature independenti su ogni commedia', while the catchwords between plays are *present*, not absent. Such variants between supposedly identical copies are not uncommon; see below, our remarks about 'binary' editions.

El pintor de su deshonra. Collation: A–B^{8} C^{6}. Paged 1–43, the last blank. The third play.

La hija del aire part II. Wrongly attributed here to Antonio Enríquez Gómez. Collation: A–C^{8}. Paged 1–47, the last blank. The sixth play.

Mr T. R. A. Mason tells us that *La desdicha de la voz*, the fourth play in *Diferentes XLIII* and the only one entirely by Calderón, collates A–C^{8} and is paged 1–48. These two volumes must have been made up to sell off a stock of unsold *sueltas*.[38a]

Bibliographers such as E. Cotarelo y Mori, A. G. Reichenberger, J. Simón Díaz and X. A. Fernández have already drawn attention to oddities in the series of *Comedias escogidas*, where a given volume exists in more than one edition, one of the editions generally being composed of *sueltas*.[39] Since we can add to Professor Fernández's information about the British Library copy of the *Sexta parte*, we describe it here:

PARTE SEXTA. | DE | COMEDIAS | DE LOS MEjORES | INGENIOS DE ESPAÑA. | [wood-block of flowers] | CON LICENCIA. | [rule in thirteen pieces] | EN MADRID.

The title-page verso is blank. π2^{r} gives the contents:

[38a] [I have since seen film of the Freiburg University Library copy of *No hay burlas con el amor*, which is of the same edition, and confirms the above guesses concerning collation and pagination (except that [p. 44] is blank). It may be added that the *sueltas* of *Diferentes XLII* can be divided into groups on the basis of recurring damaged types; the groups show signs of being the work of a single firm, although they may not be of the same date – D.W.C.]

[39] E. Cotarelo y Mori, 'Catálogo descriptivo de la gran colección de "Comedias escogidas" que consta de cuarenta y ocho volúmenes, impresos de 1652 a 1704', *Boletín de la Real Academia Española*, xviii (1931), 232–80, 418–68, 583–636, 772–826; xix (1932), 161–218; A. G. Reichenberger, 'The "Quinta Parte" of "Comedias Nuevas Escogidas"', *The Library Chronicle*, xvii (University of Pennsylvania, 1951), 115–28; for the *Sexta parte*, see J. Simón Díaz, *Bibliografía de la literatura hispánica*, iv, Madrid, 1955, items 202–3, and X. A. Fernández, 'Otra edición primitiva y olvidada de *El burlador*', in *Filología y crítica hispánica (Homenaje al profesor F. Sánchez-Escribano)*, ed. A. Porqueras and C. Rojas, Madrid & Alcalá, 1969, 243–58.

COMEDIAS QVE TIENE	eſte tomo ſexto.
No ay ſer Padre ſiendo Rey.	A–D^4.
Cada qual à ſu Negocio.	A–D^4.
El Burlador de Seuilla.	A–D^4 E^2.
Prone [sic], y Filomena.	A–D^4 E^6; foliated.
Obligados, y Ofendidos.	A–D^4 E^2.
El Eſclauo del Demonio	A–B^8 C^4 D^2; A and B misbound. Paged.
El Pleyto del Demonio con la Virgen.	A–E^4.
Los Trabajos de Iob.	A–D^4.
La Vanda, y la Flor.	A–E^4.
A vn tiempo Rey, y Vaſſallo.	A–D^4; paged.
Los Medicis de Florencia.	A–F^4.
El Principe Conſtante.	A–E^4. (pressmark 11725.b.6)

The verso of the contents-page is blank, and there are no other preliminaries. The two preliminary leaves are of different paper from the rest of the book and from each other: they are not conjugate. The tenth item is printed on paper with the Genoese coat-of-arms; this paper has retained its whiteness, but the rest of the volume is brown. The same item has no fewer than seven of the typefaces owned by Tomé de Dios Miranda in 1675, including damaged individual sorts;[40] the last page has a large wood-block used by him in the same year (see Chapter III above). The third item shows only four typefaces, all of them owned by J. F. de Blas of Seville in 1673 (our R3, R17, R26, IT7). We are reluctant, on the basis of only four faces, to make a firm attribution to a printer who bought some of his type in Madrid, but we think the date of 1673 is reliable, and that a search in Blas's other work for the damaged sorts of the large R3 COMEDIA would be worthwhile. As for the fourth and seventh items, they have two-dot js in their text-

40 The faces are our R3, R9 (with the foreign A of *sueltas* 2, 15 and 25, and the damaged A of 17 and 20), R18, R19, R34, IT4 and IT13C. R34 and IT13C have the appropriate body of 79.5 mm/20 lines.

types, and so must date from 1664–76; Seville is possible, Madrid more likely. The volume is not homogeneous, and probably dates from the mid 1670s.

The different contents of 'binary' *partes* (to use the word in the sense given currency by Wiseian scholars) may indicate that the booksellers did not have the same number of copies of all the *sueltas* they were trying to sell off, and so used substitutes (it would be no great labour to make an appropriate change in the preliminary contents-list, or even to reprint the entire preliminaries, as often happened with re-issues). Few booksellers can have had sufficient stocks of unsold *sueltas* to make up large numbers of identical volumes. This probably explains why made-up volumes of this kind generally survive in very few copies, and may explain gaps in the numbering of some series. There may well have been booksellers unscrupulous enough to invent a series with some high-sounding title, and to number their handful of made-up copies in such a way as to suggest that they formed part of this imaginary series.

Most confusing for the bibliographer are the *desglosables* which have been bound into a volume different from that for which they were designed. For example, the first edition of Tirso de Molina's *El burlador de Sevilla* appears in a *Doze comedias nuevas de Lope de Vega Carpio, y otros autores, segunda parte*, 'Barcelona, Gerónimo Margarit, 1630'. The signatures of this volume are a jumble, as is the foliation (where there is any). The text of *El burlador* is signed K–L^8 M^6, twenty-two leaves foliated 61–82. There are nine letters of the standard signature alphabet before K, but nine gatherings of eight leaves would give seventy-two, twelve leaves too many. We must therefore conclude that the volume was printed like the Cormellas *Octava parte* described above, i.e. the full signature alphabet was used, but the number of sheets per gathering varied so that each play formed a unit of its own. As it happens, two other plays in the 'Margarit' volume fit perfectly: *Marina la porquera* (Carmona), foliated 1–20, signed A–B^8 C^4, and *Deste agua no beberé* (Claramonte), foliated 41–60, signed G–H^8 I^4. A play foliated 21–40 and signed D–E^{8} F^{4}, and eight other plays, the first beginning on N1^{r}, folio 83, are needed to complete the original volume. We believe that the 'Margarit' *parte* was one of several, perhaps of many, produced in Castile during the ban of 1625–34 and given a false Barcelona imprint to disarm suspicion.

We have seen a similar example, bound in a volume of true *sueltas*: Juan Pérez de Montalbán, *El príncipe de los montes*. At one time it evidently formed part of a collected volume of plays, for its foliation begins with 147 and ends with 166, a total of twenty leaves. Had this been quired in a normal quarto volume in eights, it would have occupied two gatherings and half of a third; this play, however, collates Y–Z^{8} Aa^{4}, and while Y and Z are signed on the first five leaves, Aa is signed only on the first three, a sure sign that it is not the remnant of a dismembered eight-leaf gathering. A similar but apparently different *desglosable* of this play appeared in *Parte XXVIII*, Huesca, 1634. We are fairly certain that the print we have seen belongs to Seville, *c.* 1630.[41]

Misleading and false imprints, or fakes intended to deceive, seem to have been most common in the seventeenth century, perhaps because interest in the dramatists' work was keenest among their contemporaries. *Sueltas* began to be printed in what must have been very large numbers in the second half of the century, but there was a continuing demand for collected volumes, as we can tell from the recurrence of volumes of *sueltas* bound together in the guise of *partes*. The last major fake of this kind involved the plays of Calderón. A total of 108

[41] [This *desglosada*, formerly Professor Wilson's, is now in Cambridge University Library. I discuss it and the 'Margarit' volume of *Doze comedias nuevas* in an article ('The first edition of *El burlador de Sevilla*') due to be published in the *Hispanic Review*. *Doze comedias nuevas* was actually assembled in Seville by Simón Faxardo; parts of it, including *El burlador de Sevilla*, were the work of Manuel de Sande, also of Seville. Two other 'Barcelona' volumes mentioned below, Lope's *Parte 25* (pp. 154–5) and *Parte 27* (p. 159), are also Seville work; Manuel de Sande had a hand in both of them – D.W.C.]

titles (but considerably more *editions*) was collected and bound in nine volumes, to be passed off as the edition published by Don Juan de Vera Tassis. As we have shown elsewhere, this fake edition was probably produced in the early years of the eighteenth century.[42]

Although *partes* continued to be printed after 1700, the eighteenth century was in some respects the great age of the *comedia suelta*. Serial numbers came into use and imprints, though not universal, became commoner again. One set of *suelta* serial numbers has been shown to relate to a collection of *partes*; another has been shown to be random.[43] We suspect that most sets of serial numbers relate only to the order in which the printer happened to print the plays, but further investigation may at least determine which *sueltas* belong to which series. It should then be much easier to date the various *sueltas* in the series, either by their numbers or by the state of the type used in them. Finally it should be possible to identify the printers, even in cases where a consortium was involved.

As the eighteenth century advanced, the new writers such as Jovellanos and Fernández de Moratín also found their plays appearing in *suelta* form, but not to the exclusion of the work of Golden-Age dramatists, which continued to be printed, although less frequently, until the mid nineteenth century. Here are three examples from the period 1801–50:

[42] D. W. Cruickshank and E. M. Wilson, 'A Calderón collection in Dr Steevens' Hospital, Dublin', *Long Room*, ix (1974), 17–27. Restori noted similar but less ambitious collections of the plays of Moreto and Tirso de Molina: A. Restori, 'La collezione CC*IV. 28033 della Biblioteca Palatina-Parmense', *Studj di Filologia Romanza*, vi (1893), pp. 84 and 110.

[43] J. Moll, 'Las nueve partes de Calderón editadas en comedias sueltas (Barcelona, 1763–1767)', *Boletín de la Real Academia Española*, li (1971), 259–304; and W. T. McCready, 'Las comedias sueltas de la casa de Orga', in *Homenaje a William L. Fichter*, Madrid, 1971, 515–24. [More recently A.J.C. Bainton has found evidence for three different sets of serial numbers in the production of Antonio Sanz of Madrid; one is apparently random, the others strive to be alphabetical: 'The *comedias sueltas* of Antonio Sanz', *Transactions of the Cambridge Bibliographical Society*, VII, ii (1978), 248–54 – D.W.C.]

[L. Fernández de Moratín], *La comedia nueva, ó el cafe . . .* 4°. $1–3^{4}$, paged [1]–24. Valencia, Ildefonso Mompié, 1822.

[G. M. de Jovellanos], *El delincuente honrado . . .* 4°. $1–3^{4}\ 4^{2}$, paged [1]–28. Valencia, Ildefonso Mompié, 1822.

Francisco de Rojas, *Del rey abajo ninguno . . .* 4°. $[1]–3^{4}\ 4^{2}$, paged [1]–28. Valencia, Ildefonso Mompié de Montagudo, 1839.

The third is, of course, a Golden-Age play. All three have serial numbers, and the second and third advertise the fact that various kinds of play, new and old, may be bought from Mompié.

Within a quarter century of the date of the last of these three *sueltas*, a change took place. The British Library's copy of Bretón de los Herreros's *Achaque a los vicios* (11725.h.15) is of uncertain format, but its ten unsigned leaves are twice as large as the old quarto *sueltas*. A colophon gives the date: Madrid, 1862. More significantly, the play is preceded and followed by advertisement-lists of nearly 1000 titles, none of them positively identifiable as a Golden-Age piece.

The period which saw this change also saw the appearance of the first reliable statistics for literacy in Spain. In the mid nineteenth century, seventy-five per cent of the population could not read. There is no reason to believe that the percentage was appreciably (if at all) lower in the previous three centuries, the period of the *comedia suelta*. But if the literate were numerically and proportionally fewer, they must have been very active consumers, to have stimulated the trade as they did. Today, only a small proportion of the literate public is given to reading plays. In seventeenth- and eighteenth-century Spain the proportion was obviously much greater. The reason for this major change in reading habits is beyond the scope of our monograph. However, we do not think that the change took place in the nineteenth century: the Bretón de los Herreros '*suelta*', though different in appearance, content and perhaps literary standard, is still of the same *genre*. We suspect, therefore, that the introduction of radio (and subsequently, of films and television) was responsible. In any event, the *comedia suelta* had outlived its usefulness.

★ ★ ★ ★ ★ ★

Some years ago we suggested some differences between seventeenth- and eighteenth-century *sueltas* by comparing one play from the Guillén de Castro *parte* of 1618–21, one printed by Francisco de Leefdael's widow of Seville (*floruit* 1730–3) and one by Joseph and Tomás de Orga of Valencia, 1772.[44] In that study we considered that probably the following features were exclusive to seventeenth-century printers: 1. The use of quarto in eights in at least some gatherings; 2. The use of figurines on title-pages or under head-titles, sometimes with a profusion of compartmental borders; 3. The absence of serial numbers; 4. The continuation of the traditional uses of initial V (or v) and internal u (except in headings such as IORNADA SEGVNDA – *anglicè* Second Act) – though these conventions possibly apply to some very early eighteenth-century prints; 5. The widespread use of pica as a text-type, especially on a body of 85–8 mm/20 lines after about 1650, and the lack of small pica.

We have found so far little reason to modify these conclusions. Much remains to be done, however, particularly with regard to number 5, but we hope that we have now made a start. We still believe that pica is the most common *suelta* text-type in the seventeenth century. Although there is at least one example of a true small pica in Pepys 1553, it is used on a body of 69 mm, which in Spain is effectively a long primer (*entredós*) body. The small pica which became common in Spain in the eighteenth century averages 75 mm/20 lines (Spanish *filosofía*); the Pepys *sueltas* have no type in the range 70–9 mm. We now realise that the pica body of 85–8 mm is to be associated with Madrid or, more exactly, with Madrid typefounders. It probably denotes a *suelta* of the later seven-

[44] '*Comedias sueltas* – a bibliographical problem', in *The textual criticism of Calderón's comedias*, pp. 211–19 (see note 36).

teenth century, but it does not follow that pica of 80–4 mm is earlier than 1650. Thirty years ago, it was stated that 'as the final paragraph in the actual description of the book, the most intensive bibliographies may add a note on the typography'. A few years ago we considered this sufficient; we now think that to be of any real use, *suelta* bibliographies must be intensive, and that the more notes they add on type the better.[45]

As for number 1, we are still unable to say exactly when quartos in fours began to replace those in eights as the staple format. This is largely because there are too few seventeenth-century *sueltas* with dates that can be trusted. Some we have dated ourselves – Calderón's *Fieras afemina amor* (1670), Rojas Zorrilla's *Lucrecia y Tarquino* (1671–3),[46] and the Pepys *sueltas* (1671–83) are in fours: this seems to be the case with all *sueltas* after 1670. Those before 1650, on the other hand, seem to be in eights. So the change appears to have taken place between 1650 and 1670. At first sight it might appear to be due to setting by pages instead of by formes: Spanish printers were chronically short of type, and a move to set by pages rather than by formes would almost inevitably force many of them to change from quarto in eights to quarto in fours (eleven pages must be set to complete one forme when setting quarto in eights by pages; if in fours, only seven pages). However, we have good

45 The passage quoted is from Fredson Bowers, *Principles of bibliographical description*, New York, 1962, p. 300. This was written originally in 1949, since which, see G. T. Tanselle, 'The identification of type faces in bibliographical description', *PBSA*, lx (1966), 185–202. The necessary minimum is the body-size of the text-type, a measurement which is easily made and understood (see A. J. C. Bainton, *Comedias sueltas in Cambridge University Library: a descriptive catalogue*, Cambridge, 1977). Identifying typefaces by cutters will aid only specialists; accurate measurements of the larger titling capitals would be simpler and almost as useful for the specialist. Photographs such as we include here are best, but obviously out of the question where large collections are involved.

46 D. W. Cruickshank, 'Rojas Zorrilla's *Lucrecia y Tarquino*: the date and printer of the first known edition', *Modern Language Notes*, xcii (1977), 329–31.

reason to believe that setting by formes continued as late as 1675 in Spain.[47] Further investigation is required here.

* * * * * *

All through this account – after the periods and authors covered by Mr Norton and the late Professor Gillet – we have had to make do with much inferior bibliographical help. We have learned something from La Barrera, from Salvá and from Pérez Pastor, but their works appeared many years ago. Unfortunately Antonio Rodríguez-Moñino, whose article on Torres Naharro was most useful to Gillet, was not otherwise interested in the theatre;[48] other recent scholars such as José F. Montesinos produced excellent criticisms of Lope, but his interest was in the content, not the format, of printed books. Our chapter is therefore an outline only, or – to change the metaphor – a number of pointers to what other scholars will follow up and thoroughly work out.

47 See Cruickshank, 'Some aspects of Spanish book-production in the Golden Age', *The Library*, V, xxxi (1976), p. 3, especially note 11.

48 A. Rodríguez-Moñino, 'El teatro de Torres Naharro', *Revista de Filología Española*, xxiv (1937), 37–82.

CHAPTER FIVE

Bibliographical Descriptions and Notes

To save space in this section, we use the following abbreviations:

Aguilar Piñal: Francisco Aguilar Piñal, *Impresos sevillanos del siglo XVIII*, Madrid, 1974.

Bainton: A. J. C. Bainton, *Comedias sueltas in Cambridge University Library: a descriptive catalogue*, Cambridge, 1977.

Chorley: John Rutter Chorley (1807?–67), poet and scholar, born at Blackley Hurst, Lancashire. 'He devoted himself especially to the Spanish drama, and formed a superb collection of plays, which he partly gave, partly bequeathed to the British Museum. The enumeration of his manuscript notes in separate dramas occupies between six and seven columns of the museum printed catalogue' (*Dictionary of National Biography*).

Cruzada Villaamil: G. Cruzada Villaamil, 'Teatro antiguo español. Datos inéditos que dan a conocer la cronología de las comedias representadas en el reinado de Felipe IV', *El averiguador*, i (1871), 7–11, 25–7, 73–5, 106–8, 123–5, 170–2, 201–2.

La Barrera: C. A. de la Barrera y Leirado, *Catálogo bibliográfico y biográfico del teatro antiguo español*, Madrid, 1860.

Medel: F. Medel del Castillo, *Índice general alfabético de todos los títulos de comedias*, ed. J. M. Hill in *Revue Hispanique*, lxxv (1929), 144–369.

Moll: J. Moll, *Catálogo de comedias sueltas conservadas en la Biblioteca de la Real Academia Española*, Madrid, 1966.

Moll/Calderón: J. Moll, 'Las nueve partes de Calderón editadas en comedias sueltas (Barcelona 1763–1767)', *Boletín de la Real Academia Española*, li (1971), 259–304.

Moll/Orga: J. Moll, 'La serie numerada de comedias de la imprenta de los Orga', *Revista de Archivos, Bibliotecas y Museos*, lxxv (1968–72), 365–456.

Morley and Bruerton: S. G. Morley and C. Bruerton, *The chronology of Lope de Vega's comedias*, London & New York, 1940 (revised Spanish version, Madrid, 1968).

N. Carolina: W. A. McKnight and M. B. Jones, *A catalogue of the comedias sueltas in the Library of the University of North Carolina*, Chapel Hill, 1965.

Oberlin: P. P. Rogers, *The Spanish drama collection in the Oberlin College Library – a descriptive catalogue*, Oberlin (Ohio), 1940.

Palau: A. Palau y Dulcet, *Manual del librero hispano-americano*, 2nd ed., Barcelona, 1948 (vol. i) – 1976 (vol. xxvii). (In course of publication, volume xxviii to be the last.)

Paz y Melia: A. Paz y Melia, *Catálogo de las piezas de teatro que se conservan en el Departamento de Manuscritos de la Biblioteca Nacional*, 2nd ed. by J. Paz, Madrid, 1934–5.

Pennsylvania: J. M. Regueiro, *A catalogue of the comedia collection in the University of Pennsylvania Libraries*, New Haven (Connecticut), 1971.

Profeti: M. G. Profeti, *Per una bibliografia di J. Pérez de Montalbán*, Verona, 1976.

Rennert: H. A. Rennert, 'Notes on the chronology of the Spanish drama', *Modern Language Review*, ii (1906–07), 331–41; iii (1907–08), 43–55.

Restori: A. Restori, *Saggi di bibliografia teatrale spagnuola*, Geneva, 1927.

Salvá: P. Salvá y Mallén, *Catálogo de la biblioteca de Salvá*, Valencia, 1872.

Toledo: E. Juliá, 'Comedias raras existentes en la Biblioteca Provincial de Toledo', *Boletín de la Real Academia Española*, xix (1932), 566–83; xx (1933), 252–70.

Toronto: J. A. Molinaro, J. H. Parker and E. Rugg, *A biblio-*

graphy of comedias sueltas in the University of Toronto Library, Toronto, 1959.

Wayne State: B. B. Ashcom, *A descriptive catalogue of the Spanish comedias sueltas in the Wayne State University Library and the private library of Professor B. B. Ashcom*, Detroit, 1965.

Whitney: J. L. Whitney, *Catalogue of the Spanish library and of the Portuguese books bequeathed by George Ticknor to the Boston Public Library*, Boston, 1879.

B.L.: British Library (*olim* British Museum).

B.N.M.: Biblioteca Nacional, Madrid.

E.M.W.: in the library of Professor E. M. Wilson [and now in U.L.C.].

U.L.C.: University Library, Cambridge.

With the exception of Bainton and Profeti, the *suelta* catalogues listed above are too brief in their descriptions to make identification certain. That of Regueiro (Pennsylvania) is particularly brief, being intended only as an index to a microfilm collection of the originals (we have therefore compared photographs of the Pepys *sueltas* with the Pennsylvania microfilms, and noted the two occasions (*sueltas* 6 and 12) where the Pennsylvania collection has another copy of the Pepys editions). One of the most important parts of the Pennsylvania collection is twenty-four bound volumes of *sueltas* formerly owned by the Harrach family. With the exception of volume 24, most of these *sueltas* were probably collected in Spain in the latter part of the seventeenth century.[1] Those which are not the same as the Pepys ones are quite likely to be contemporary with them, so we have indicated their provenance and volume

[1] See A. G. Reichenberger, 'The Counts Harrach and the Spanish theater', *Homenaje al profesor Rodríguez-Moñino*, Madrid, 1966, vol. ii, pp. 97–103.

number in the manner (Harrach 1).[2]

[Since this chapter was written, two major new works have appeared: Mildred V. Boyer, *The Texas collection of comedias sueltas: a descriptive bibliography*, Boston, 1978; and K. and R. Reichenberger, *Bibliographisches Handbuch der Calderón-Forschung*, vol. i, Kassel, 1979. Professor Boyer very kindly sent us pages from her typescript, and this information has been incorporated below. The Drs Reichenberger also very kindly sent us a great deal of information, which was incorporated likewise. Volume i of their *Handbuch* contains some new Calderón or pseudo-Calderón *sueltas*, which I have decided not to add (but compare their items 3099–3101, 982–92, 552–6, 2927–8 and 3192–5 with our numbers 6, 9, 10, 21 and 22). Their third volume, soon to appear, will contain detailed *suelta* descriptions – D.W.C.]

Pepys 1553(1), pp. 1–36 · *Gaselee*, 7 · *Palau* 22350

EL PREMIO EN LA TIRANIA. | COMEDIA | FAMOSA, | *Por Don Franciſco Balcarcel y Lugo.* | Hablan en ella las perſonas ſiguientes. | [Persons in italics – two columns] | [rule] | [two large Ws,

[2] We should like to thank the following for their generous assistance in the preparation of this monograph: Mr R. C. Latham, CBE, the Pepys Librarian and Mrs E. M. Coleman, Assistant Librarian, of Magdalene College, Cambridge; Mr N. J. Barker, Dr D. E. Rhodes and Mrs M. Johnson of the British Library; Dr P. Gaskell of Trinity College, Cambridge; Mr J. C. T. Oates, FBA, Mr F. J. Norton and Mr A. J. C. Bainton of the University Library, Cambridge; Professor V. F. Dixon of Trinity College, Dublin; the Drs K. and R. Reichenberger of Kassel; Dr H. D. L. Vervliet of the Plantin-Moretus Museum, Antwerp; Mr A. R. A. Hobson; Miss A. E. Harvey Wood of the National Library of Scotland; Mr B. Scarfe of La Trobe University, Victoria; and Professor Mildred V. Boyer of the University of Texas at Austin. Finally, we are particularly grateful to Lionel and Philip Robinson for their financial assistance. [For the works of Mr Norton, the Drs Reichenberger and Professor Boyer from which we were sent details prior to publication, see p. 86, n. 2 and the added paragraph above.]

sideways, as ornament] JORNADA PRIMERA. [two large Ws, sideways, as ornament]

[Begins] *Correfe vna cortina, y aparece Conftantino | fentado en vna filla, fojeando libros, que | eftaràn fobre vn bufete.*

Conft. TIrana crueldad, qué intentas?
Refolucion del deffeo, . . .

4°. A–D4 E2. No page numbers.

[Running headlines – verso] *EL PREMIO EN LA TIRANIA.*

[Running headlines – recto] *POR D. FRANCISCO BALCARCEL Y LVGO.*

[Catchwords] A4v: *Emp.* B4v: mal C4v: que D4v: de

[Ends] del premio en la tirania
perdonad yerros tan grandes.
F I N.

[At the foot of the right-hand column on the last page is a poem headed:]

Octauas en alabança del Autor defta Come-|dia, por don Iuan Serot, Doctor en | Sacra Theologia.

Docta Vniuerfidad, y con razon,
Vueftra Comedia pues, la confidero;
Por enredos en ella vn Calderon, . . .

[two *octavas reales*]

[Juan Cabezas, *c.* 1675–78]

Earlier history unknown. La Barrera lists the author under Valcarcel (p. 412a) but mentions only this play.

Later *suelta* in the British Library: 11728.a.32: Valladolid, Alonso del Riego, n.d. (B.L. guess-date: ?1750). This omits the poem in praise of the author.

Pepys 1553(2), pp. 37–68 · *Gaselee*, 116

SAN FRANCO DE SENA, | COMEDIA FAMOSA, | *DE DON AGVSTIN MORETO.* | Hablan en ella las perfonas figuientes. | [Persons in italics – four

columns] | [line of ornaments M1]
[Begins] IORNADA PRIMERA. | *Dizen dentro Franco, y Aurelio.*
Fr. No huyais, que yo ſolo ſoy.
A. Algũ diablo es q̃ eſperamos. . . .
4°. A–D4. No page numbers.

[Running headlines – verso]	*San Franco de Sena*	A1v.
	San Franco de Sena.	All but A1v, D2v.
	San Franco de Seua.	D2v.
[Running headlines – recto]	*Comedia famoſa.*	All but A2r, B1r, B4r, C1r, D1r.
	Comedia Famoſa.	A2r, B4r.
	San Franco de Sena.	B1r, C1r, D1r.

[Catchwords] A4v: *Dat.* B4v: torpe C4v: la
[Ends] dâ fin dichoſo a San Franco
de Sena, Lego del Carmen.
[four ornaments M17] F I N. [four ornaments M17]
[Tomé de Dios Miranda, *c.* 1675]

First printed in the *Primera parte de comedias escogidas*, Madrid, 1652. Printed with the title *El lego del Carmen* in Moreto's *Primera parte* of Madrid, 1654 (reprinted at Valencia in 1676, Madrid in 1677). The Bibliothèque Nationale, Paris, lists two copies of a *suelta* (?) of five quarto gatherings, Valencia, B. Macé, 1676 (Yg.250[10] and Yg.253[10]).

B.L.: two *sueltas*, 11728.h.18(13) of ?1730, and 1342.e.13(3) of ?1770.

University of Texas, 103.16: n.p., n.d., 32 pp., serial number 38.

Pennsylvania: two imprintless editions: 618 (Harrach 9) and 2811; a third of the eighteenth century: 1659.

N. Carolina: two imprintless editions: 1615 and 1616.

Wayne State: two imprintless editions: 491a, 491b.

Moll: two imprintless editions, 1035, 1036.

U.L.C.: imprintless *suelta*, serial number 252 (Bainton 732).

E.M.W.: *suelta* in pseudo-Moreto *Primera parte*, Salamanca, Imprenta de la Santa Cruz, n.d.
Toledo: imprintless *suelta*, 20 leaves, serial number 116 (as Moll 1036): Juliá xx, 266.
Aguilar Piñal: three copies of an undated *suelta* (early eighteenth century) by the heirs of Tomás López de Haro, Seville: 1533.
Suelta printed by the widow Orga, Valencia, 1765: Bainton 733, Toronto 597, Oberlin 4717, Wayne State 491c, Moll 1037.
Chorley's note in B.L. 11728.h.18(13): 'Con título de *"El lego del Carmen"*, insertóse esta obra en la P[te] 1 de las Comedias de Moreto, Madrid 1654 y con el de nuestra edición en la 1 de las *Escogidas* (1652). Segun Fernandez-Guerra "debería titularse mas bien *San Franco de Sena*: vease el *Speculum Carmelitanum* de 1680 del Padre Daniel de la Virgen Maria, impreso en Amberes año de 1680: t. 2. pte. 789." Con razon la estima este critico "monstruosa en el plan, pero llena de bellezas admirables."'

According to N. D. Shergold and J. E. Varey ('Some palace performances of seventeenth-century plays', *Bulletin of Hispanic Studies*, xl [1963], 237), there was a performance of this play by Manuel de Vallejo, probably on 7 December 1631, paid for on 21 December of that year.

This play is available to modern readers in the *Comedias de Moreto* in the *Biblioteca de Autores Españoles*, xxxix, first printed in 1865. Frank P. Casa studies it in the first chapter of his *The dramatic craftsmanship of Moreto*, Cambridge (Massachusetts), 1966, pp. 7–29.

A *refundición* by José Estremera, with music by Arrieta, was first played in the Teatro de Apolo, Madrid, on 27 October 1883. This version was published in the same year (see Oberlin 2186).

Pepys 1553(3), pp. 69–103 · *Gaselee*, 109

LOS LAGOS | DE SAN VICENTE. | ACTO PRIMERO. | PERSONAS. | [Persons in italics – four columns]

[Begins – initial stage-direction crosses the page] *En lo alto de vnos riſcos Paſqual villano muy à lo groſſero con vn baſton, y vna honda.* | *Por la mitad de los riſcos el Rey Don Fernando de caza.*

Paſ. HAo? Que eſpantays el cabrio;
verá por do ſe metio! . . .

4°. A–D4 E2. A2 mis-signed D2. 1–35 pages. Last page blank.

[Running headlines – verso]	*Los lagos de S. Vicente.*	All pages but those listed below.
	Los lagos de San Vicente.	A1v, B1v, C3v.
	Los Lagos de S. Vicente.	A4v, B3v, C1v, D1v, D4v.
[Running headlines – recto]	*del M. Tirſo de Molina.*	A2r.
	Del M. Tirſo de Molina.	All others.

[Catchwords] A4v: vengan- B4v: Templa C4v: de D4v: quien

[Ends] ſon eſtos, en la ſegunda
Tirſo ſu fin os promete.
FIN.

[Tomás López de Haro, *c.* 1683]

Printed in Tirso's *Quinta parte de las comedias*, Madrid, 1636. E. W. Hesse ('Catálogo bibliográfico de Tirso de Molina', *Estudios*, v [1949], 809) quotes four *sueltas*, one n.p., n.d., three of Seville (Padrino, 1700?; no printer, 172–?; Correo Viejo [Leefdael or his widow, *c.* 1700–33]).

B.L.: *sueltas* 11728.d.62 (Seville, ?1740); and 11728.i.21(1) (Seville, Joseph Padrino, ?1700) [= second Hesse item?]

Aguilar Piñal, two *sueltas*: Lucas Martín de Hermosilla, n.d. (1482), and Joseph Padrino, n.d. (1483); the second item is also recorded as Moll 598. Aguilar Piñal and Escudero agree that Padrino began printing in 1748, so the guess 1700? is wrong.
N. Carolina 1007: Seville, J. A. de Hermosilla, n.d.
Pennsylvania 727: n.p., n.d. (Harrach 18).
U.L.C., Bainton 437: n.p., n.d.
E.M.W.: Seville, Padrino, n.d.
Bibliothèque Nationale, Paris: n.p., n.d. (8° Yg. Pièce.696), '4°, A–D'.
Oberlin 6864: Seville, Correo Viejo, n.d. [= last Hesse item?]; 6865: n.p., n.d.

In the second of the B.L. *sueltas* Chorley wrote:

'Hallase en la P^{te} V de las Comedias de Tirso: Madrid, 1636.

No sabemos si llegó á componerse la II^{a} Parte que promete el Poeta en los versos finales de esta: – por lo menos si escribiole, no se ha conservado hasta nuestros dias.

Sobre el asunto de esta Comedia hé aqui lo que dice Salazar de Mendoza (Monarquia de España III. tom. Madrid, 1770. Ibarra.) hablando del reynado de D. Fernando, primer Rey de Castilla (1031–1067).

"Fue tambien" (en su tiempo) "la ida de Sta Casilda hija del rey Almenon de Toledo, Christiana, a lo menos *in voto*, a bañarse al Lago de S. Vicente, cerca de Briviesca en Bureva, para guarecerse del fluxo de sangre que padecia: al sanar de él, y quedarse á vivir en aquella tierra en una casilla que labró junto á las fuentes del Lago. Tienese con esta Santa mucha devocion por toda la Comarca de Burgos: – y por eso hay muchas mugeres con su nombre." Tit^{o} V del Lib. 2. Cap. I. Tom. I. 127.'

The play was reprinted in the second volume of Doña Blanca de los Ríos's edition of the *Obras dramáticas completas* of Tirso de Molina (Fray Gabriel Téllez), Madrid, 1952, pp. 12–52. Her study of the play is not very rewarding.

Pepys 1553(4), pp. 105–36 · *Gaselee*, 112 · *Palau* 176955

LA SIRENA DEL IORDAN | SAN JVAN BAPTISTA. | COMEDIA | FAMOSA. | DE DON CRIS TOVAL [sic] DE MON ROY. [sic] | y Silva. | Habla [sic] en ella las perſonas ſiguientes. | [Persons in three columns, italics] | [line of 13 ornaments M1] | JORNADA PRIMERA.
[Begins] *Sale Zacarias de barba, al trage Sacer-|dotal, y dos, ô tres criados miniſiros* [sic] | *del Templo.*
Zac. Monarca Omnipotente,
gran Sabaot, a quien continuamẽte . . .
4°. A–D4. No page numbers.
[Running headlines – verso] *La Sirena del Iordan San Iuan Baptiſta.* All but C1v, D1v.
La Sirena del Iorda. Snn Iuan Bapʇiſta. C1v.
La Sirena del Iordan San Iua Baptiſta. D1v.
[Running headlines – recto] *Comedia famoſa.* All but A3r, B3r.
Comedia Famoſa. A3r, B3r.
[Catchwords] A4v: Zabu- B4v: das C4v: en [wrong catchword]
[Ends] pido perdon de las faltas,
quãdo a vueſtros pies me poſtro,
[hand M7] F I N. [hand M7]
[Final ornament W1]
[Tomé de Dios Miranda, *c.* 1678]
Printed in *Parte* 45 of the *Comedias nuevas escogidas*, Madrid, 1679.
B.L. *suelta*: 11728.i.4(18) of Seville, Joseph Padrino, ?1760, which may be the same edition as N. Carolina 1677 and Aguilar Piñal 1508.
B.N.M. MS/18.074, Paz y Melia 3396, has a work of the same

title described as 'Comedia de Monroy', but the incipit is different. Paz y Melia detects the hand of Francisco de Rojas on the first leaf, when he wrote: 'Señor San Bautista.' 'Diferente.' He adds that Durán gave it an alternative title, *El lucero del sol*, of which there was an unpublished manuscript. We have not seen the *suelta* in the Bibliothèque Nationale, Paris ('Comedia famosa de San Juan Bautista . . . Valladolid, A. del Riego, n.d.'): Yg.351(12).

Pepys 1553(5), pp. 137–68 · *Gaselee*, 176

LA CREACION DEL MVNDO, | y primera culpa del hombre. | (***) | COMEDIA | FAMOSA, | *DE LOPE DE VEGA CARPIO.* | Perſonas que hablan en ella. | [Persons in italics – three columns] | ([Line of ornaments M2]) | JORNADA PRIMERA.

[Begins] *Suena muſica dentro, y deſcubreſe vn | trono muy bien adereçado, al lado de-|recho San Miguel, con eſpada, y eſcudo, | y al ſinieſtro Luzbel, ambos con | tunicelas.*

Mig. QVè atrevidos penſamiẽtos,
loco, rebolviendo eſtás? . . .

4°. A–D4. No page numbers.

[Running headlines – verso]		
	La Creacion del mundo,	All but A4ᵛ, B2ᵛ, C3ᵛ, C4ᵛ, D1ᵛ, D3ᵛ, D4ᵛ.
	La Creacion del mundo.	A4ᵛ, B2ᵛ, C3ᵛ, C4ᵛ, D1ᵛ.
	LOA.	D3ᵛ.
	LOA	D4ᵛ.

[Running headlines – recto] *y primera culpa del hombre* All but A2^{r}, B2^{r}, D4^{r}.
y primer aculpa del hombre A2^{r}, B2^{r}.
LOA D4^{r}.

[Catchwords] A4^{v}: co- B4^{v}: *Abel.* C4^{v}: cu-

[End of play on D3^{r}] primera culpa del hombre
principio de males tantos.

[Another work begins in the middle of D3^{r}]

LOA SACRAMENTAL.

En el inſtante primero
que crió el Auguſto Ceſar . . .

[Ends] *Ambos.* Porque de aqueſte modo ſe | convenga
vn zelo vueſtro, y vna dicha | nueſtra.

F I N.

[Final ornament W2 on D4^{v}]

[Juan Cabezas, *c.* 1676–9]

Morley and Bruerton place this work among the 'Plays of doubtful authenticity' – it probably is not by Lope. Chorley in a manuscript note in B.L. 11728.h.6(15) says:

'Es esta una de las piezas que cita Nicolas Antonio, como comprendidas en la P^{te} XXIV de Lope: Madrid 1640: la cual segun parece anda perdida el dia de hoy.

Hallase un MS (traslado) de una pieza asi titulada en la Biblioteca del Señor *Durán*, con el nombre de Luis Velez de Guevara, y es posible ser la misma que aqui, asi como en el libro de *Comedias nuevas*: Amsterdam *1726*: se atribuye á Lope.'

The last cited work is *Comedias nuevas de los mas celebres Autores, y realzados Ingenios de España* . . . En Amstardan [sic], A Costa de David Garcia Henriquez, 1726, pp. 129–56, *desglosable* it collates A–C^{4} D^{2}. According to the contents of the Pennsylvania copy of a Lope *Parte 23*, Valencia, M. Sorolla, 1629 (Pennsylvania 2321), it is the fifth play in that volume.

This is not the 'usual' Lope *Parte 23* of Madrid, María de Quiñones, 1638, and Morley and Bruerton refer only to the 1640 *Parte 24* of Madrid.

The play by Luis Vélez is now in B.N.M. (MS/15.047); there is a modern edition by Henryk Ziomek and Robert White Linker, Athens (Georgia), 1974. There appear to be many *suelta* editions of the play attributed to Lope:

B.L.: 1072.h.3(5), n.p., n.d., guess-date ?1650; 11728.f.59, Barcelona, Juan Centené and Juan Serra, n.d.; 11728.h.6(15), Salamanca, Imprenta de la Santa Cruz, n.d.; anonymous, 11726.f.23, n.p., n.d., guess-date ?1760.

Aguilar Piñal: 1747, Lucas de Hermosilla, n.d.; 1748, Joseph Padrino, n.d.

N. Carolina: 442, Joseph Padrino, n.d. (as second Aguilar Piñal item?); 443, Salamanca, Santa Cruz, n.d. (as third B.L. item?); 444, Barcelona, Centené and Serra, n.d. (as second B.L. item?); 445, Madrid, Antonio Sanz, 1744.

Oberlin: 7129, Madrid, Juan Sanz, n.d.

Pennsylvania: 512, n.p., n.d. (Harrach 1); 2482, Barcelona, Centené and Serra, n.d. (as B.L. and N. Carolina?).

Toronto 597, Wayne State 116 and Bainton 185 also record Barcelona, Centené and Serra, n.d.

E.M.W.: Salamanca, Santa Cruz, n.d. (as B.L. and N. Carolina?).

Bibliothèque Nationale, Paris: 8° Yg.1308(68), n.p., n.d. ('4°, A–D').

Whitney: p. 392b, n.p., n.d., 12 leaves.

Imprintless U.L.C. *suelta*: Hisp.5.76.30[8], n.p., n.d. Guess-date ?1750 (Bainton 184).

Despite the late guess-date given to this U.L.C. *suelta* by the Cambridge University Library cataloguers of 1910, the piece seems to us possibly of the seventeenth century and to merit a special description:

[Head title] LA CREACION DE EL MUNDO, | Y PRIMER CULPA DE EL HOMBRE. | COMEDIA FAMOSA, | *DE UN INGENIO DE ESTA CORTE.*

| Hablan en ella las perſonas ſiguientes.
+ + *San Miguèl.* + + *Eva.* + + *Lamec.* + +
+ *Luzbel.* + *Caìn.* + *Tubal.* +
+ + *Adan.* + + *Abèl.* + + *Seth.* + +
[rule in ¿13? sections])(g)(JORNADA PRIMERA.)(g)(
[Note on types. The letters 'U' in MUNDO, CULPA and in *UN* are crude and foreign additions to the faces concerned. The words COMEDIA FAMOSA are set in R13, except for the As of FAMOSA, which are R9.]
[Begins] *Suena muſica dentro, y deſcubreſe un trono* | *muy bien aderezado, al lado derecho San* | *Miguèl con eſpada, y eſcudo, y al* | *lado izquierdo Luzbel, ambos* | *con tunicelas.*
Mig. Quì atrevidos penſamientos,
loco, revolviendo eſtâs? . . .
[The query here (and in many other places) is an inverted semicolon.]
4°. A–B⁴ [C]². Paged: [1] 2 [3] 4–6 [7–8] 9–11 [12] 13–20
[Running headlines – verso] *LA CREACION DEL MUNDO.* All but [C]1ᵛ, [C]2ᵛ.
LA CREACION DEL MUNDO [C]1ᵛ.
LA CREACION DE EL MUNDO. [C]2ᵛ.
[Running headlines – recto] *DE VN INGENIO DE ESTA CORTE.* [hybrid *V*] All but A4ʳ, B4ʳ, [C]2ʳ.
DE VN INGENIO DE ESTA CORTE. [*V* normal] A4ʳ, B4ʳ, [C]2ʳ.
[The second *I* in *INGENIO* is barely readable on A3ʳ, B3ʳ.]
[Catchwords] A4ᵛ: debe- B4ᵛ: y
[Ends] primera culpa del hombre
principios de males tantos.
FIN.

[No colophon] [Text in small pica, 74 mm/20 lines; italic *è* frequent in roman, but note *ì* for è in first word of text; italic proper is actually Haultin's *médiane italique grasse* (see Chapter III, note 41), worn and impure.]

We have not been able to identify the 'Loa sacramental' in Pepys 1553(5). The play is available to modern readers in the third volume of Menéndez y Pelayo's edition of the *Comedias* of Lope de Vega. His preface to the play is worth attention as is the study by Edward Glaser, entitled 'Lope de Vega's *La creación del mundo y primera culpa del hombre*', *Annali dell'Istituto Universitario Orientale (Sezione Romanza)*, iv, no. 1 (1962), 29–56.

Pepys 1553(6), pp. 169–200 · *Gaselee*, 29

[Double line of ornaments M4] | EL ESCLAVO DE MARIA. | COMEDIA FAMOSA. | DE DON PEDRO CALDERON. | Interlocutores. | [Persons in italics – three columns] | [line of ornaments M5] | JORNADA PRIMERA.

[Begins] S*ale Feniſa, y Don* I*uan.*
Fen. Eſtraña reſo ucion! [sic]
d.Iu. Como la juzgas eſtraña, . . .

4°. A–D4. No page numbers.

[Running headlines – verso]	El Eſclavo de Maria.	All but B1v, D2v.
	De Don Pedro Calderon.	B1v, D2v.
[Running headlines – recto]	De Don Pedro Calderon.	All.

[Catchwords] A4v: vn pa- B4v: mañana C4v: ani-

[Ends] el dichoſo eſclavo
menor de Maria. FIN.

[Tomé de Dios Miranda, *c.* 1678]

In his *Parte IV* of 1672 Calderón denied that he wrote this play. Its title does not occur in the list of his authentic works submitted by Francisco Marañón to Charles II of Spain, nor in that which the poet sent to the Duke of Veragua.[3] Vera Tassis included it in the list of plays spuriously attributed to Calderón, printed as *sueltas* (*Verdadera quinta parte*, Madrid, 1682, fol. ¶¶7ᵛ). The play was presumably in print before 1672, so the eighteenth-century dramatist's play with the same title (Don Juan Bernardino Rojo – see La Barrera, pp. 343–4) cannot be this one. Salvá, i, 598b–599a, says that he has a *suelta* 'de mediados del siglo XVII'. La Barrera also mentions ?another play with the same title by Francisco de Villegas and Jusepe Rojo on p. 494. And under Diamante he lists as a *comedia suelta La devocion del Rosario, ó El esclavo de María ó El defensor del Rosario*. 'Impresa en 1672.' (p. 124b). Aguilar Piñal lists two *sueltas* under Diamante, but they belong to the eighteenth century: 1328, *La devoción del Rosario y el esclavo de María*, Joseph Padrino, n.d.; 1329, *La devoción del Rosario*, Francisco de Leefdael, n.d.

Three imprintless *sueltas*: B.L., 11728.b.12, ?Madrid, ?1740; Moll 396; Whitney, p. 49a. Pennsylvania 666 (Harrach 13) is another copy of the Pepys *suelta*.

Pepys 1553(7), pp. 201–32 · *Gaselee*, 106

EL PREMIO DE LA VIRTVD, Y SVCESSOS | PRODIGIOSOS DE DON PEDRO GVERRERO. | COMEDIA | FAMOSA, | DE DON ANTONIO DE MENDOZA. | Hablan en ella las perſonas ſiguientes. | [Persons in italics – three columns] | JORNADA PRIMERA.

[3] The Veragua list is most readily available in Hartzenbusch's edition of Calderón's *Obras*, vol. i, pp. XXXIX–XLII (vol. vii of the *Biblioteca de Autores Españoles* series); for the Marañón list, and its relation to the Veragua and Vera Tassis lists, see E. M. Wilson, 'An early list of Calderón's *comedias*', *Modern Philology*, lx (1962), 95–102.

[Begins] *Salen Iuan Guerrero viejo, y Pedro Guerre-|ro ſu hijo, veſtidos de labradores, y Pedro | Guerrero con vnas coplas.*
Iuan Gue. Bien medrarè deſſa ſuerte,
pues quando te embiò [sic] á arar . . .
4°. A–D4. No page numbers.
[Running headlines – verso] DE DON PEDRO GVERRERO,
All but C1v, D3v.
DE DON PEDRO GVERERRO,
C1v, D3v.
[Running headlines – recto] EL PREMIO DE LA VIRTVD,
Y SVCESSOS PRODIGIOSOS
[Catchwords] A4v: *d.Die.* B4v: con C4v: ſe
[Ends] donde veas con mi muerte
de ſus Reynos los ſuceſſos.
FIN.
[Tomás López de Haro, *c.* 1678–83]

See G. A. Davies, 'A chronology of Antonio de Mendoza's plays', *Bulletin of Hispanic Studies*, xlviii (1971), 100: *suelta*, n.p., n.d., B.N.M.: T/20.666. 'The loose construction and lack of technical skill point to early composition . . . this *comedia* may have been Mendoza's earliest venture into the theatre.' The play is not included in Antonio Hurtado de Mendoza's *Obras liricas, y comicas, divinas, y humanas* of 1728, although there is another *suelta* in Toledo. Juliá's description (xx, 261) is contradictory: sixteen leaves, but A–E4. Medel listed a *Premio de la virtud,* which he ascribed to D. Pedro Guerrero!

Pepys 1553(8), pp. 233–64 · *Gaselee*, 184

LA AVRORA DEL SOL DIVINO. | COMEDIA FAMOSA | *DE FRANCISCO XIMENEZ SEDEñO.* | Hablan en ella las perſonas ſiguientes. | [Persons in italics – three columns] | IORNADA PRIMERA.
[Begins] *Salen Aminadob* [sic] *Mayoral, y Liſeno,* | *labrador.*

Ami. A quien no admira Liſeno,
la honeſtidad de MARIA. . . .
4°. A–D4. No page numbers. No running headlines.
[Catchwords] A4v: los B4v: ſi C4v: para
[Ends] *Ami.* Y aqui ſe queda Senado,
la Aurora del Sol Divino.
[ornament M6] F I N. [ornament M6]
[Juan Francisco de Blas, *c.* 1673]

La Barrera (199b): 'Escribió un soneto á la muerte de Perez de Montalban. (*Lagrimas panegíricas.* – Madrid, 1639.) *La Aurora del sol divino.* Schack cita una comedia de este título, manuscrita, con la licencia fechada en 1640 y bajo el nombre de Francisco de Monteser.' Salvá, i, 572b: 'Tengo dos ediciones bastante antiguas con el nombre de este autor.'

The manuscript is in the B.N.M.: MS/16.621: 'Al fin de la primera jornada la firma y rúbrica del autor, y al pie de la página: En Ciudad Real, Francisco de Montes. Al terminar la segunda, la firma y rúbrica de Sedeño, y al final de la comedia: Licencia fechada en Málaga 1637: otra de Madrid 1640 (?) que parece de mano de Tirso de Molina, y con su rúbrica.' Paz y Melia, i, 302.

Moll 106: Salamanca, Imprenta de la Santa Cruz, n.d.

Pennsylvania 582, n.p., n.d. (Harrach 6).

Bibliothèque Nationale, Paris (under Sedeño): Seville, J. Navarro y Armijo, n.d. (8° Yg.Pièce.374); n.p., n.d. (8° Yg.Pièce.373). Both listed as 8° [sic].

Pepys 1553(9), pp. 265–312 · *Gaselee*, 30

LA GRAN COMEDIA. | DE LA EXALTACION DE LA CRVZ. | DE DON PEDRO CALDERON. | PERSONAS. | [Persons in italics – two columns] | [rule in eleven sections] | IORNADA PRIMERA.

[Begins – initial stage direction crosses the page] *Salen Siroes, y Menardes, Principes de Perſia, cada vno por ſu puerta,* |

repreſentando al teatro, que ha de ſer vna montaña.
Sir. Hà del ſoberuio monte,
que linea deſigual deſte Orizonte, . . .
4°. A–F4. No page numbers. Running headlines savaged by binder's knife.
[Running headlines – verso] La Exaltacion de la Cruz.
Where readable.
[Running headlines – recto] De Don Pedro Calderon.
Where readable.
[Catchwords] A4^v: el B4^v: IOR- C4^v: *Arro-* D4^v: ni E4^v: para
[Ends] la Exaltacion de la Cruz,
perdonad ſus muchos yerros.
FIN.
[Possibly Tomé de Dios Miranda, *c.* 1671]

There is a manuscript copy of the play in the B.N.M., with licences for performance in Madrid dated 25 October 1662, and in Saragossa, 26 November 1662 (Paz y Melia, 1353; E.M.W., 'Calderón and the stage-censor in the seventeenth century', *Symposium*, Fall 1961, 172–3). The play is not mentioned in the list of Francisco Marañón nor in that of the Duke of Veragua (see note 3 above), but in both lists Calderón mentioned another title: *El triunfo de la Cruz*, which may conceivably refer to this play. The play was first printed in the first volume of the *Comedias escogidas*, Madrid, 1652; as Calderón wrote the *aprobación* for this volume we can safely accept the play as his own (see E.M.W., 'Seven *aprobaciones* by Don Pedro Calderón de la Barca', *Studia philologica – Homenaje ofrecido a Dámaso Alonso*, iii [1963], 605–18). As the play mentions a royal marriage to a king's niece and a plea to the king to lend his troops to escort his bride, the play was probably composed during the 1640s and performed after the theatres reopened when Mariana of Austria was due to arrive in Madrid. The play was reprinted by Vera Tassis in his *Parte VII* of 1683 (see the note by Hartzenbusch in *Biblioteca de Autores Españoles*, xiv, 663–5). Vera Tassis listed *El triunfo de la cruz* among the 'manuscritas' in his vol. VII; in his vol. IX of 1691 he announced that it would form part of his vol. X, never published.

Dr Kurt Reichenberger of Kassel has informed us by letter that the Pepys print is probably identical with the following five *sueltas*: one in the Biblioteca Nazionale at Florence in the pseudo-*Primera parte de escogidas* described by A. Gasparetti, *Archivum Romanicum*, xv (1931), 560–71; one in the Niedersächsische Staats- und Universitätsbibliothek at Göttingen (8° Poet. dram. II 82–2[12]); one in the Österreichische National-Bibliothek at Vienna (442.278–B); one in the Biblioteca Apostolica Vaticana at Rome (R.G. Lett.est. IV 300.int.2); and one in the Biblioteca Marciana at Venice (Dramm. 3905.1).

We also know or have been told of the following *sueltas*: Pseudo-Vera Tassis *Parte VII*: B.N.M., R/11351(4); Steevens' Hospital Library, Dublin, H.5.8(4); D. W. Cruickshank's copy, also fourth play in the volume. These are all copies of the same edition, as is the differently-bound London Library copy, P.1052(14). Another pseudo-Vera copy in Pennsylvania (956) may differ. None of these has imprint or date.

Without imprint or date but with the serial number 207 and 32 pages:

B.N.M., T/3.153; Biblioteca Menéndez Pelayo at Santander, 130; Stadtbibliothek, Mainz, VI f.67(3).

Seville, Joseph Padrino, n.d.: B.N.M., T/32.018 (Aguilar Piñal 1198); Bibliothèque Municipale, Montpellier, V.12.204; Freiburg Universitätsbibliothek, Comedias sueltas, Bd. 6; University of Texas, 21.44.1; N. Carolina 764; E.M.W.

Valladolid, Alonso del Riego, n.d.: B.N.M., T/7.158; Real Academia de la Historia, Madrid.

Madrid, Imprenta de la calle de la Paz [Antonio Sanz?], 1728: Pennsylvania 2692.

Barcelona, Pedro Escuder, 1760: Berkeley, 787t. T252.v.3(20).

Barcelona, Carlos Sapera, 1764: E.M.W.

Barcelona, Carlos Sapera and Francisco Suriá, 1766: N. Carolina 765; B.N.M., T/14.646[8]; Biblioteca Universitaria de Barcelona (Moll/Calderón).

Barcelona, Francisco Suriá and Carlos Sapera, 1771: Moll 419; Bibliothèque Nationale, Paris, 4° Yg.21(67); E.M.W.; B.N.M., T/5.025 and T.14.813(18); Bainton 326; Whitney, p. 50b (probably, although he does not mention Suriá or Sapera).
Salamanca, Imprenta de la Santa Cruz, n.d.: B.L., 11726.c.1(9), guess-date ?1780.

The play is available both in the second volume of Hartzenbusch's edition of Calderón's works in the *Biblioteca de Autores Españoles* (vol. ix of the whole collection) and also in the volume entitled *dramas* edited by Ángel Valbuena Briones (Madrid, 1959).

Pepys 1553(10), pp. 313–44 · *Gaselee*, 28

LAS CADENAS DEL DEMONIO. | COMEDIA FAMOSA. | *DE DON PEDRO CALDERON.* | Hablan en ella las perſonas ſiguientes. | [Persons in italics – three columns] | [rule] | JORNADA PRIMERA.

[Begins] *Sale Yrene, Flora, y Siluia deteniendola.*

*Yre.*Dexadme las dos. *Flo.*Señora.
mira. *Sil.*Oye. *Flo.*Aduierte.
*Yre.*Que tengo . . .

4°. A–D4. All leaves signed. No page numbers.

[Running headlines – verso] Las cadenas del Demonio.

[Running headlines – recto] De don Pedro Calderon.

[Catchwords] A4^{v}: *Ceu.* B4^{v}: lle- C4^{v}: *Rey.*

[Ends] dando fin a ſu Comedia
con el perdon de ſus faltas?
F I N.

[1650–84, ?Seville]

The authenticity of this play is doubtful. The title does not occur in either the Marañón or in the Veragua lists (see note 3, p. 136). The play is rather a poor one. The title is quoted in a farce (the *Entremés del doctor Carlino*), printed in 1648 (Emilio

Cotarelo y Mori, *Ensayo sobre la vida y obras de D. Pedro Calderón de la Barca*, Madrid, 1924, pp. 280–2). In 1682 – a year after Calderón's death – Vera Tassis listed it in the preliminaries to the *Verdadera quinta parte* under the heading: 'Las que estàn impressas sueltas.' He printed it in the *Parte VIII* of 1684. The Pepys copy – if it was brought back to England from Seville in February or March 1684 – probably antedates the Vera Tassis volume, whose *suma de la tassa* is dated 13 October 1684.

Dr Kurt Reichenberger has told us of what appears to be another copy of this *suelta*. Formerly (i.e., before the war) in the Preussische Staatsbibliothek, it is now preserved in the Preussischer Kulturbesitz, West Berlin, pressmark Xk 1482–2(9). He has also sent xerox prints of a *suelta* bound in the Göttingen volume described above under Pepys 1553(9): 8° Poet. dram. II 82–2(5). The Göttingen *suelta* greatly resembles Pepys 1553(10). The type is the same. It too is fully signed (A, A2, A3, A4, etc.) throughout. The planning of the head-title, incipit and running headlines are also similar throughout. On the first page we noticed these differences:

Pepys	Göttingen
JORNADA	IORNADA
Yrene	*Irene*
Yre	*Ire*

There is in the British Library a collection of '13 Comedias Nuevas | Parte novena | De D^{n} Pedro Calderon'. In it is the bookplate of 'The Honble Frederick North' (? i.e. Frederick, Lord North, 1732–92). Its pressmark is C.108.bbb.20 – *olim* 1072.h.9. The eleventh *suelta* in this volume is another copy of the Göttingen one. The printed catalogue's guess-date for the B.L. copy is: ?Madrid, ?1700. However, in view of the similarity between the two editions (type, layout, page-for-page correspondence), we believe that both are the work of one firm, and produced about the same time (that is, the B.L. catalogue's guess underestimates the age of the *suelta*, and is almost certainly wrong in suggesting that it was printed in Madrid). On the other hand, we are not convinced that a single compositor setting up a second edition from one he had set earlier would regularly (and apparently deliberately) change the spelling of the name Yrene/Irene. For this reason (as stated earlier), we are not certain that the habit of signing all four leaves in a quarto gathering was that of one compositor in particular (in any case, signatures were frequently added by someone other than the compositor who had set the pages).

There are of course other *sueltas* too; first, those without date or imprint: Pseudo-Vera Tassis *Parte VIII*: B.N.M., R/11.352(5); Pennsylvania 969; Steevens' Hospital Library, Dublin, H.5.9(5); Bainton 118; Wayne State 77a; University of Texas, 21.19.1. (These are not all of the same edition.)
Also without date or imprint, but with serial number 26: B.N.M., T/2.106, T/14.782(7); Moll 149, 150; Oberlin 986; Österreichische National-Bibliothek, Vienna, 443.646-B; University of California, Calderón, Comedias 20; Freiburg Universitätsbibliothek, Comedias sueltas, Bd. 5; Glasgow University Library, 86.d.3; Bainton 119; National Library of Scotland, Edinburgh, Ag.4/69(2). (Many of these references were sent by Dr Kurt Reichenberger. We have managed to compare the Scottish National Library *suelta* with Bainton 119: they differ, so there must be at least two editions with the number 26. The Scottish National Library one is almost certainly of Madrid, *c.* 1700–10.)
B.L., 11728.h.16(18); London Library, P.1051(2), guess-date ?1760.
Pennsylvania 515 (Harrach 1) and 661 (Harrach 13).
Wadham College, Oxford, X.12.13(12).
Those with date and/or imprint:
Barcelona, Francisco Suriá and Carlos Sapera, 1766: B.L., 11725.ee.4(9); B.N.M., T/3821; Biblioteca Universitaria de Barcelona (Moll/Calderón); Bibliothèque Nationale, Paris, 4° Yg.21(114); New York Public Library, NPP p.v.1, no. 4.
Barcelona, Francisco Suriá y Burgada, n.d.: N. Carolina 277; E.M.W.; Moll 151; Wayne State 77c; Oberlin 985; Santander,

Biblioteca Menéndez Pelayo, 356; Venice, Biblioteca Marciana, 110.C.26.7; Wellesley College, Massachusetts, Coe Library; two copies in the collection of Mr Bruno Scarfe, La Trobe University, Victoria, Australia.[4]

The play is reprinted in the third volume of Calderón's plays edited by Juan Eugenio Hartzenbusch in the *Biblioteca de Autores Españoles* (volume xii of the series) and in that entitled *dramas* of Ángel Valbuena Briones (Madrid, 1959).

Pepys 1553(11), pp. 345–76 · *Gaselee*, 47

El Jvramento Ante Dios, | Y Lealtad Contra El Amor. | comedia famosa, | Del Alferez Jacinto Cordero. | Hablan en ella las perſonas ſiguientes. | [Persons in italics – two columns] | [rule]

[Begins] JORNADA PRIMERA. | *Tocan caxas, y ſalen algunos ſoldados, el* | *Conde Vitorino, coronado de Laurel,* | *y Perelo.*

Cond. NO toquen ſonoras caxas,
ni beliſonas trompetas, . . .

4°. A–D4. No page numbers.

[Running headlines – verso] *El juramento ante Dios, y lealtad contra el amor.*
All but A1v, A2v, B4v, C3v, D2v, D4v.
El juramento ante Dios y lealtad contra el amor.
A2v.
El juramento ante Dios, y lealtad contra el amor,
A1v, B4v, C3v.

4 See B. Scarfe, 'Seventeenth- to nineteenth-century editions of Spanish drama: a personal collection', *Bulletin of the Comediantes*, xxix (1977), 126–35.

Comedia famoſa, del Alferez Iacinto Cordero.
D2^{v}, D4^{v}.

[Running headlines – recto] *Comedia famoſa, del Alferez Iacinto Cordero.*
All but D1^{r}, D3^{r}.
El juramento ante Dios, y lealtad contra el amor.
D1^{r}.
El juramento ante Dios, y lealtad contra el amor,
D3^{r}.

[Catchwords] A4^{v}: *Beat.* B4^{v}: pues C4^{v}: *Duq.*

[Ends] por propio nombre, y cũplido
el juramento ante Dios.
F I N.

[Widow of Nicolás Rodríguez, 1671–4]

According to José Simón Díaz's *Bibliografía de la literatura hispánica*, iv, 1955, item 202, this play appeared as no. 7 (16 unnumbered leaves) in a set of *sueltas* with printed title-page entitled *Sexta parte de comedias escogidas, de los mejores ingenios de España*, Saragossa, heirs of Pedro Lanaja y Lamarca, 1653. Cotarelo also lists this volume in his 'Catálogo descriptivo . . .', pp. 262–6 (see note 39, p. 112 above). Neither Cotarelo nor Simón Díaz gives a location, but Cotarelo had probably seen the Toledo copy described by Juliá (xix, 569–70). La Barrera (p. 705) knew of a copy in the then Imperial Library at Vienna; it is still there, although the institution is now the Österreichische Nationalbibliothek. The two copies may not be identical. This *Sexta parte* should not be confused with that produced by the same printers in Saragossa in 1654 (also preserved in Vienna, see La Barrera, p. 689), or with the 'Madrid' *Sexta parte* of *c.* 1675 which we have described above (pp. 112–13).

The play also appeared in *Parte quarenta y quatro de comedias de diferentes autores*, Saragossa, heirs of Lanaja y Lamarca, 1652 (i.e. the same printers). From Salvá's description (i, 1184) this was also a volume of *sueltas,* but the play had 36 pages. Profeti ('Appunti bibliografici . . .', pp. 178–80—see note 21, p. 102) lists two variants of this edition, although both contain our play.

Cordero was born in Lisbon, and some catalogues call him Cordeiro. There are many *sueltas* of this play:

Madrid, Antonio Sanz, 1740: B.L., 11726.e.1(3); N. Carolina 1001.

Madrid, no printer, 1746: B.L., 11728.h.13(13).

Madrid, Antonio Sanz, 1753: Biblioteca Municipal, Madrid; Santiago de Compostela, Biblioteca Universitaria; N. Carolina 1002; Wayne State 272a; Oberlin 1620.

Barcelona, J. Piferrer, n.d.: Pennsylvania 2906.

Seville, F. de Leefdael, n.d.: Palau 61776.

Seville, widow of F. de Leefdael, n.d.: Aguilar Piñal 1308.

Barcelona, Pedro Escuder, 1756: Biblioteca Municipal, Madrid.

Madrid, no printer, 1770: Palau 61776.

Valencia, J. and T. de Orga, 1781: Biblioteca del Instituto del Teatro, Barcelona (Moll/Orga 243); Wayne State 272b.

Barcelona, F. Suriá y Burgada, n.d.: Toronto 354; Moll 591.

Madrid, Quiroga, 1796: Bainton 435; Moll 592; B.L., 1342.e.8 (13).

The following have no imprint: B.L., 11728.c.13, 11728.f.100 (9) (two copies, guess-date ?1720); Moll 590; Pennsylvania 540 (Harrach 3).

Pepys 1553(12), pp. 377–408 · *Gaselee*, 154

LA SEGVNDA MAGDALENA, | Y SIRENA DE NAPOLES. | COMEDIA | FAMOSA. | DE DON FRANCISCO DE ROXAS. | Hablan en ella las perſonas ſiguientes | [Persons in italics – three columns] | [line of ornaments M5, M7, M8] | IORNADA PIMERA. [sic]

[Begins] *Salen huyendo Criſpin, y Ceſar loco con | vn palo, y Fabio tras ellos.*

Criſ. Guarda el loco, que aſſegura
para dar *Ceſ.* Si el ſeſſo pierdo . . .

4°. A–D4. No page numbers.

[Running headlines – verso] La ſegunda Magdalena, y Sirena de Napoles. All but A4v, B4v, C2v, D2v.
La ſegunda Magdalena, y Sirena de Napoles, A4v, B4v, C2v, D2v.

[Running headlines – recto] De Don Franciſco de Roxas.

[Catchwords] A4v: *Marg.* B4v: *Iuſt.* C4v: mis

[Ends] cuya hiſtoria es en Italia
venerada, y verdadera.
F I N

[Tomé de Dios Miranda, *c.* 1675]

There appears to be no reference to this play in La Barrera. Raymond R. MacCurdy lists *sueltas*, and describes the play as apocryphal (R. R. MacCurdy, *Rojas Zorrilla: bibliografía crítica*, Cuadernos bibliográficos, no. 18, Madrid, 1965, p. 30). Medel gives two plays entitled *Segunda Magdalena*, one attributed to D. Francisco de Roxas, another to D. Juan Bautista Diamante. Under Diamante, however, La Barrera lists a play called *La Magdalena de Roma y bella Catalina* (p. 124b): cf. the *suelta* at Pennsylvania (2781), *La Magdalena de Roma Cathalina la bella*, Madrid, A. Sanz, 1748, which is attributed to Diamante.

There are two imprintless *sueltas* of the pseudo-Rojas play in the B.L.: 11728.f.11 (guess-date ?1700) and 11728.h.21(7) (guess-date ?1710). Pennsylvania 708 (Harrach 15) is another copy of the Pepys *suelta*.

MacCurdy lists (besides the Pepys *suelta*):

n.p., n.d. (siglo XVII) – Arturo Sedó, Barcelona [now in the Biblioteca del Instituto del Teatro, Barcelona].

n.p., n.d., British Library ?= 11728.f.11 or 11728.h.21(7)?

N. D. Shergold and J. E. Varey ('Some palace performances of seventeenth-century plays', p. 238) record a performance of a play called *La serena de Napoles* by Juan de Morales at Aranjuez, paid for on 5 May 1625. Cruzada Villaamil and Rennert read *Sirena* for *serena*.

Pepys 1553(13), pp. 409–40 · *Gaselee*, 171

LA AZVZENA DE ETIOPIA. | COMEDIA FAMOSA, | *DE D. FRANCISCO DE LA TORRE.* | Hablan en ella las perſonas ſiguientes. | [Persons in italics – four columns] | [rule] | [two hands M9] JORNADA PRIMERA. [two hands M9]

[Begins] *Subeſe vna cortina, y deſcubreſe la mitad de | vn glovo por la parte inferior, que es la tierra, | compueſta de yervas, flores, y edificios, y ſalen por vn lado Medùſa, y por otro | Fineo de gala.*

Med. Salve, ſoberano Rey.
Fin. Salve, Monarca ſupremo . . . .

4°. A–D4. No page numbers. No running headlines.

[Catchwords] A4v: Re- B4v: pues C4v: *Sef.*

[Ends] la Azuzena de Etiopia.
Victoria, victoria.
F I N.

[Juan Cabezas, *c.* 1676–9]

First printed in Don Francisco de la Torre y Sebil's *Luzes de la aurora*, Valencia, Geronimo Villagrasa, 1665, pp. 474–532. The first act is by Don Iosef de Bolea, the second by Don Francisco de la Torre, the third was begun by Bolea and completed by Torre. The text includes a *loa* (pp. 469–73) by Bolea and a *Moxiganga de fiestas, y fiesta de moxigangas* (pp. 503–14) not reprinted in this *suelta*. There is a manuscript of this play in the B.N.M. (Paz y Melia, 334) which describes the work as a 'Comedia y auto [sic] de tres ingenios, don José Bolea, D. Francisco de la Torre Sevil? y D . . .?' [sic] (MS/16.844). This is clearly an old mistake. According to Paz y Melia the manuscript dates from the end of the seventeenth century.

We know of no other *suelta* of this play.

Pepys 1553(14), pp. 441–71 · *Gaselee*, 51

EL MEjOR REY DEL MVNDO, | Y TEMPLO DE SALOMON. | COMEDIA FAMOSA. | DE ALVARO CVBILLO. | Hablan en ella las perſonas ſiguientes. | [Persons in italics – three columns] | [line of ornaments M10] | IORNADA PRIMERA.

[Begins] *Suena muſica, corren cortina de vna ca-|ma en que eſta el Rey David acoſtado,* | *con barba larga, y Berſabà* [sic] *Reyna,* | *en el eſtrado como hablando.*

Da. Ya Berſabè de mi palabra dada,
  vueſtros ojos veran el deſempeño, . . .

4°. A–D4. Last page blank. No page numbers. No running headlines.

[Catchwords] A4^{v}: por B4^{v}: mas C4^{v}: *Arm.*

[Ends] *Bañ.* Y aſsi, Senado
  queda a ſegunda parte combidado.

[ornament M6] FIN. [ornament M6]

[Juan Francisco de Blas, *c.* 1673]

Early *suelta* in the B.L.: T.1736(10), guess-date ?Madrid, ?1640:

Fol.I. | EL MEjOR REY DEL MVNDO, Y TEMPLO DE SALOMON, | COMEDIA | FAMOSA. | De Aluaro Cubillo. | Hablan en ella las perſonas ſiguientes. | [Persons in three columns, italics] | [rule] | IORNADA PRIMERA.

[Begins] *Suena muſica, corrẽ cortina de vna ca|ma en q̃ eſtà el Rey Dauid acoſtado cõ barba larga, Betſabe Reyna en el* | *eſtrado, como hablando* | *con el.*

Dau. Ya, Betſabe, de mi palabra dada
  vueſtros ojos veran el deſempeño, . . .

4°. A–D4. Foliated, but too indistinctly to read. Last page blank.

[Running headlines – verso] *El mejor Rey del mundo, y Templo de Salomon.*
  All but A2^{v}, B4^{v}, C2^{v}.

El meyor Rey del mundo, y Templo de Salomon.
A2ᵛ, B4ᵛ, C2ᵛ.

[Running headlines – recto] *De Aluaro Cubillo.*
[Catchwords] A4ᵛ: eſpoſa B4ᵛ: de C4ᵛ: [?]diſi-
[Ends] fama eterna le dan.
Baña Y aſsi el Senado
queda a ſegunda parte combidado.
F I N.
[No colophon]

According to Fajardo (quoted by La Barrera, p. 440), the play was printed in a Lope *Quinta parte* of Seville or Madrid, 1634. There is another *suelta* which corresponds closely with T.1736(10) – B.L., 11728.c.21, guess-date ?1700. Salvá, i, 623a, records another *suelta*, but with no details. Also Pennsylvania 547, n.p., n.d. (Harrach 3) and Moll 749, n.p., n.d., serial number 196.

Pepys 1553(15), pp. 473–504 · *Gaselee*, 108

EL CONDENADO POR DESCONFIADO. | COMEDIA FAMOSA | DEL MAESTRO TIRSO DE MOLINA. | Hablan en ella las perſonas ſiguientes. | [Persons in italics – four columns] | [line of ornaments M1, M7]
[Begins] JORNADA PRIMERA. | *Sale Paulo de Ermitaño.*
Pau. Dichoſo alvergue mio,
ſoledad apacible, y deleitoſa, . . .
4°. A–D⁴. No page numbers.
[Running headlines – verso] *El Condenado por deſconfiado.*
All but A2ᵛ, A4ᵛ, B2ᵛ, C4ᵛ, D2ᵛ.
El Condenado po deſconfiado.
A2ᵛ, B2ᵛ, C4ᵛ, D2ᵛ.

Comedia ſamoſa.

A4^{v}.

[Running headlines – recto] *Comedia ſamoſa.*

[Catchwords] A4^{v}: ſal B4^{v}: que C4^{v}: ô

[Ends] y pena, y gloria trocadas,
el cielo os guarde mil años.

F I N.

[Tomé de Dios Miranda, *c.* 1678]

This play is now generally accepted as an authentic play by Tirso de Molina (Fray Gabriel Téllez), although its authorship has been disputed. It was first printed in the *Segunda parte de las comedias del Maestro Tirso de Molina . . .*, Madrid, 1635. It is often considered the greatest of all Spanish 'theological dramas'.

There is a late (1824) but interesting manuscript in the Biblioteca Municipal, Madrid, described by D. Rogers in 'El manuscrito de "El condenado por desconfiado"', *Homenaje a William L. Fichter*, Madrid, 1971, pp. 659–71. Rogers also refers to three *sueltas*:

n.p., n.d.: Royal Library, Copenhagen (probably the earliest).

Francisco Sanz, Madrid, n.d. (he printed in the last third of the seventeenth century): Biblioteca Municipal, Madrid.

n.p., n.d., serial number 232: three copies, all in B.N.M. (T/15284, T/14993^{14} and T/14990^{9}).

There is also Pennsylvania 670, n.p., n.d. (Harrach 14); the B.L. (11728.d.57, guess-date ?Seville, ?1740); and the Bibliothèque Nationale, Paris (n.p., n.d., Yg.345[11], 'Impression du XVIIe s.').

There are many modern editions of the play, the best of them that of D. Rogers (Oxford, 1974). There are too many studies of it to be listed here.

Pepys 1553 (16), pp. 505–36 · *Gaselee*, 118

GVARDAR PALABRA A LOS SANTOS. | COMEDIA FAMOSA. | De Don Sebaſtian de

Olivares. | Hablan en ella las perſonas ſiguientes. | [Persons in italics – two columns]

[Begins] IORNADA PRIMERA. | *Sale Ariſta de camino ſantiguandoſe.*

Ari. Iamàs huvo aſſombro igual,
ni cupo en lo varonil, . . .

4°. A–D4. No page numbers. No running headlines.

[Catchwords] A4ᵛ: y el B4ᵛ: *Ariſt.* C4ᵛ: *Leo.*

[Ends] le dè ſu Autor fin dichoſo,
ſi es que os merece el perdon.
*** F I N. ***

[Seville, *c.* 1671–2, possibly Tomé de Dios Miranda or Juan Francisco de Blas]

This play was printed in the *Parte veinte de comedias varias nunca impressas* . . ., Madrid, 1663. We know of two other *sueltas,* both different from ours, although not necessarily from each other: Toledo (Juliá, xx, 254: A-D4 E2, 18 leaves) and Pennsylvania 588, n.p., n.d. (Harrach 7). Escudero (2909) lists a *suelta* printed in Seville by L.M. de Hermosilla, but it has not been seen since.

Pepys 1553(17), pp. 537–68 · *Gaselee,* 111

EL GIGANTE CANANEO. | COMEDIA | FAMOSA. | DE DON CHRISTOVAL DE MONROY | Y SILVA. | Hablan en ella las perſonas ſiguientes. | [Persons in italics – two columns] | JORNADA PRIMERA.

[Begins] *Tocan chirimias, y ſalen el Rey de Licia* | [tear] *quilina dama, y Niceta, con todos los* | *hombres, y mugeres que pudieren de acom|pañamiento, y muſicos cantando, y todos* | *coronados de guirnaldas de ramos* | *y flores.*

Muſic. LA deicad [sic] de Iupiter ſanto
aplauſos reciba, . . .

4°. A–D4. No page numbers.

[Running headlines – verso] *El Gigante Cananeo.*
[Running headlines – recto] *De Don Chriſtoval de Monroy.*
All but A3^r, B2^r, C3^r.
De Don Chriſtaval de Monroy.
A3^r, B2^r, C3^r.
[Catchwords] A4^v: y B4^v: ſi en C4^v: *Can.*
[Ends] a errado ſuplan deſſeos
el defecto de las obras.
F I N.
[Tomé de Dios Miranda, *c.* 1678]

See Paz y Melia 2306: '*El mayor vassallo del mayor señor (El gigante Cananeo, San Cristóbal)* . . . Escrita, según nota, al fin de la primera jornada, en Sevilla, por Pedro Vallés, en 4 de julio de 1658.' (MS/15.220). We know of the following *sueltas*:
B.L., 11728.i.4(14), n.p., n.d., guess-date ?Madrid, ?1710.
Whitney (p. 233b), Seville, n.d.
N. Carolina 857, Madrid, Antonio Sanz, 1729.
Bibliothèque Nationale, Paris, Yg.351(11), Madrid, Antonio Sanz, 1729 (as N. Carolina 857?)
Aguilar Piñal 1500, Seville, Francisco de Leefdael, n.d.
Scarfe collection, La Trobe University: Madrid, Antonio Sanz, 1744 (see note 4, p. 144).
Moll 478, Seville, Joseph Padrino, n.d. (listed as Aguilar Piñal 1501).
Oberlin 4591, Seville, Joseph Padrino, n.d. (as Moll 478?).
Pennsylvania 651, n.p., n.d. (Harrach 12).

There is a note by Chorley in the B.L. *suelta*: 'Hallase MS en la Biblioteca de D. Agustín Durán [i.e. now in the B.N.M., MS/15.220] . . . y el titulo: – *El mayor vassallo del Mayor Señor* (Medel) ó el *Gigante Cananeo: S. Christoval* (Barrera 263). Fax[ard]o *"El mejor vassallo del mejor Señor."*'

Gerald E. Wade has a note on this author in the *Bulletin of the Comediantes*, v (1953), 3–9, 32.

Pepys 1553(18), pp. 569–604 · *Gaselee*, 175

EL ANIMAL PROFETA. | COMEDIA | FAMOSA. | DE LOPE DE VEGA CARPIO | Hablan en ella las perſonas ſiguientes. | [Persons in italics – four columns] | JORNADA PRIMERA.

[Begins] *Sale Irene ſola con vn papel en la mano.*

Iren. Jardin hermoſo, y rico,
que en belleza compites . . .

4°. A–D4 E2. No page numbers.

[Running headlines – verso] *El Animal Profeta.* All but A3v, B3v, D3v.
El Animal Pantoja. A3v, B3v, D3v.

[Running headlines – recto] *De Lope de Vega Carpio.*

[Catchwords] A4v: y ad- B4v: *Fed.* C4v: Por- D4v: vn

[Ends] patillas, ſe vean el dia
que Partieren deſte mundo.
F I N.

[Final ornament W3]

[Tomás López de Haro, 1678–83]

Morley and Bruerton state (p. 257) that the play existed only in *sueltas* in the seventeenth century. They refer to a manuscript in the B.N.M. (Paz y Melia, 221; MS/16.961) of the early eighteenth century, where this play is described as 'Comedia del Dr Mira de Amescua'. They classify the play as 'Of doubtful authenticity . . . the play, if Lope's, has been recast.' There are two other manuscripts recorded by Paz y Melia (*loc. cit.*): one of the seventeenth century (MS/14.980), the other in various hands of 1631 (MS/16.899). His note 'Impresa en la Parte 5a de las *Comedias* de Lope, Sevilla' may well refer to a collection of *sueltas*. Perhaps he is quoting La Barrera (p. 440) who, in turn, is quoting Fajardo's reference to a Lope *Quinta parte* of Seville (or Madrid), 1634 (see notes on Pepys 1553[14] above); La Barrera gives the title as *'El Dichoso patricida. (El animal Profeta, San Julian.)'*. Cf. Pennsylvania 2369, *El animal profeta, y dichoso patricida*, in a Lope *Parte 25*, Barcelona, Cormellas,

1631 (the text is of the same play, but the volume is a made-up one).[5]

We know of the following other *sueltas*:
Salvá, i, 570b.
Moll 72, n.p., n.d. *(El animal profeta, San Julian).*
Pennsylvania 2464, n.p., n.d. *(El animal profeta, San Julian).*
N. Carolina 131, Salamanca, Santa Cruz, n.d. As E.M.W.'s copy?
Bibliothèque Nationale, Paris, Yg.352(1) and Yg.358(6), both n.p., n.d. (listed under Lope and Mira); also 8° Yg.1308(35), Valladolid, A. del Riego, n.d.; and 8° Yg.1308(43), Salamanca, Santa Cruz, n.d. (under Lope).

Shergold and Varey record a performance by Juan de Morales on 24 June 1630, paid for on 13 January 1633; and a performance of '*San Julián*' on 26 June 1636, payment 26 May 1637 ('Some palace performances of seventeenth-century plays', pp. 217 and 237).

The play is available to modern readers in volume iv of Menéndez y Pelayo's edition of Lope's *Comedias.* His study of the play is worth attention. We have not seen the edition prepared by Bonnie Wilds, Barcelona, 1976, in which the play is attributed to Mira de Amescua.

Pepys 1553(19), pp. 605–36 · *Gaselee*, 132

EL DIVINO PORTUGUES | SAN ANTONIO DE PADUA. | COMEDIA FAMOSA, | *DEL DOCTOR JVAN PEREZ DE MONTALVAN.* | Hablan en ella las perſonas ſiguientes. | [Persons in italics – four columns] | [rule] | [two hands M12] JORNADA PRIMERA. [two hands M12]

[5] See V. G. Williamsen, 'Lope de Vega: a "missing" *parte* and two "lost" *comedias*', *Bulletin of the Comediantes,* xxv (1973), 42–51. Professor Williamsen's description reveals that the text of *El animal profeta* has 20 unnumbered leaves, apparently signed A–B[8] C[4]. [For *Parte 25*, see p. 115, n. 41 above.]

[Begins] *Deſcubreſe vn Oratorio, y en èl Fernando | Eſtudiante que es San Antonio, en vna | ſilla con vn libro.*

Ant. GRande fineza de amor
fue en la Mageſtad Diuina, . . .

4°. A–D4. No page numbers.

[Running headlines – verso] *El Diuino Portuguès San Antonio de Padua.* All but A1^{v}, B1^{v}.
El Diuino Portuguès San Autonio de Padua. A1^{v}, B1^{v}.

[Running headlines – recto] *Del Doctor Iuan Perez de Montalvan.*

[Catchwords] A4^{v}: como B4^{v}: ſe te C4^{v}: porque

[Ends] pues ſabeis nueſtros deſſeos,
que ſon todos de ſerviros.
F I N.

[Juan Cabezas, *c.* 1676–9]

Professor Victor F. Dixon of the University of Dublin has sent us some useful notes on this play; see also his article 'Juan Pérez de Montalbán's *Segundo tomo de las comedias*', *Hispanic Review*, xxix (1961), 91–109, especially pp. 103–5. He points out that this play, included in Montalbán's *Segundo tomo* of 1638 (reprinted in 1652 at Valencia), is a slightly variant version of the B.N.M.'s MS/15.222, which 'lacks very few lines which are to be found in *Segundo tomo*, but has over 280 which are not; and in as many as four places it tells us . . . "D^{n} Bernardino de obregon conpusso esta comedia de el dibino portugues San Antonio de Padua en 27 de julio de MDCXXIII"'. The incipit and ending of this manuscript are that of Pepys 1553(19), see Profeti, p. 430, item a).

Paz y Melia, 1074, describes another play with the same title by Fray Antonio Fajardo y Acevedo, 'ermitaño en la villa de Carcagente', an autograph dated 5 May 1683, MS/14.883. It begins with the line: *León.* Dóite el parabién, Violante.

A third play with the same title, attributed also to Montalbán, is that described by G. W. Bacon in *Revue Hispanique*, xxvi (1912), 414. Editions of it are listed by Profeti, pp. 143–4, 433–7.

The *Segundo tomo* text (that of our *suelta*) was discussed in an interesting study by Edward Glaser, 'El divino portugués San Antonio de Padua de Juan Pérez de Montalbán', *Estudios hispano-portugueses*, Valencia, 1957, pp. 133–77.

Profeti notes the existence of other *sueltas* of the *Segundo tomo* play besides the Pepys one: Bainton 255 is another, rather battered copy of Pepys 1553(19), but U.L.C.'s guess-date is ?1750 (!); B.N.M., R/11.263, n.p., n.d.; Real Academia Española, 41–IV–59(10), n.p., n.d.; Biblioteca dell'Università, Bologna, A.V.Tab.I.MI.162, vol. xxii, n.p., n.d.; she also records two *sueltas* in the Biblioteca Municipal, Madrid, and in the University Library, Barcelona, which she was not able to examine. We can add Pennsylvania 625, n.p., n.d. (Harrach 10), which is of the *Segundo tomo* text. Two other Pennsylvania prints, 740, n.p., n.d. (Harrach 19), and 1753, Salamanca, Santa Cruz, n.d., are of the other version (i.e., that described by Bacon). It may be noted that Signora Profeti describes (pp. 143–4) one edition of this other version which consists of four gatherings of four leaves each, all of them signed; this is the edition described by Restori on p. 8, and which forms part of the curious made-up *Parte XXXXXVII*, 'Valencia, 1646', which we referred to in Chapter III in connection with Pepys 1553 (10), *Las cadenas del demonio* (see p. 68).

Pepys 1553(20), pp. 637–68 · *Gaselee*, 178

EL MILAGRO POR LOS ZELOS. | COMEDIA | FAMOSA. | DE LOPE DE VEGA CARPIO. | Hablan en ella las perſonas ſiguientes. | [Persons in italics – two columns] | [line of ornaments M5, M7, M8] | IORNADA PRIMERA.

[Begins in central position on page] *Salen el Rey, y Don Alvaro, y acompañamiento.*

Rey. Dexadme todos, dexadme.

Alv. Deſpejemos cavalleros, . . .

[The first two lines are irregular – the passage is in *octavas reales*]
4°. A–D4. No page numbers.
[Running headlines – verso] El milagro por los zelos.
All but A3v.
De Lope de Vega Carpio.
A3v.
[Running headlines – recto] De Lope de Vega Carpio.
All but A2r.
El milagro por los zelos.
A2r.
[Catchwords] A4v: Y B4v: en- C4v: *d.Iuan.*
[Ends] ſegunda parte Senado,
dad perdon a la primera
F I N.
[Tomé de Dios Miranda, *c.* 1675]

Morley and Bruerton note that this play was printed only in *sueltas* in the seventeenth century. They 'regard the play as of very doubtful authenticity' (pp. 313–14) and they place it among the 'Texts not by Lope' on p. 375.

See Paz y Melia 2382, *El milagro por los celos y excelente portuguesa Doña Beatriz de Silva.* Comedia de Tirso de Molina. It begins: *Rey.* Oh, qué proposición tan importuna . . . Two manuscripts are described: MS/16.435 and MS/16.402. Both are written and signed by 'Cortés'. Who was he? The differing first line has the right number of syllables and rhyme to fit the defective opening stanza of Pepys 1553(20), in which Doña Beatriz de Silva takes part (i.e. the manuscripts are probably of the same play as our *suelta*).

Salvá had seen a *suelta* – i, 624a. A number of collections have one printed by Carlos Sapera, Barcelona, 1770: N. Carolina 1197; Toronto 435; Moll 758; Pennsylvania 2494 and 2657; Bainton 545 (two copies); Bibliothèque Nationale, Paris, 8° Yg.1341(2); University of Texas, 144.9.2. These are probably not all of one edition, since Oberlin has two different settings by Sapera, both ostensibly of 1770 (7137–8). That listed by

Whitney (p. 394a) merely as Barcelona, 1770, is probably one of them. Moll lists another (757), imperfect, but different from his 758. Another Bibliothèque Nationale *suelta*, 8° Yg.1308(47), n.p., n.d., has four quarto gatherings, like Pepys 1553(20). A text entitled *El marques de las Navas*, in a Lope *Parte 27*, 'Barcelona [but Seville?], Cormellas, 1633' (Pennsylvania 2399), has the running-title *El milagro por los celos*, and is really another edition of our play. Another rare print, although it is ostensibly a century later, is recorded by Professor Boyer: University of Texas, 144.9.1, Antonio Sanz, Madrid, 1733.

Shergold and Varey ('Some palace performances of seventeenth-century plays', p. 230) record the payment for a performance by Andrés de la Vega on 31 March 1627. The date of the performance in question is unknown.

Pepys 1553(21), pp. 669–700 · *Gaselee*, 27

EL ANGEL DE LA GVARDA. | COMEDIA | FAMOSA. | DE DON PEDRO CALDERON. | Hablan en ella las perſonas ſiguientes. | [Persons in italics – three columns] | [line of ornaments M5, M7, M8] | JORNADA PRIMERA.

[Begins] *Salen Carlos, y Paſquin.*
Car. Si es la viba [sic] natural,
  tan caduca fantaſia. . . .

4°. A–D4. D2 mis-signed C2. No page numbers.

[Running headlines – verso] El Angel de la Guarda.
All but A2^{v}, A4^{v}.
De Don Pedro Calderon.
A2^{v}, A4^{v}.

[Running headlines – recto] De Don Pedro Calderon.
All but A3^{r}.
El Angel de la Guarda.
A3^{r}.

[Catchwords] A4^{v}: le B4^{v}: *Poſ.* [sic, for *Paſ.*] C4^{v}: con

[Ends] los ſuplicais por los deſſeos,
ſi ſon prendas que lo valen.

F I N.

[Final ornament W1]

[Tomé de Dios Miranda, *c.* 1675]

Chorley has a note in B.L. 11728.h.14(19):

'Esta pieza, que no es de Calderón, siendo una de las que *Vera Tasis* pone en la lista de "Supuestas que andaban Sueltas debaxo de su nombre". – Parece ser la misma que se halla en la P^te^ VI (furtiva) de *Escogidas*, de Zaragoça 1653 (Münch Bellinghausen 55.) la cual Barrera, (415) afirma ser la Obra asi titulada de Valdivielso, incluyda en el libro "*Doze Autos Sacramentales y Dos Comedias Divinas*: Por el Maestro Joseph de Valdivielso. 4to. *Toledo*. Por Juan *Ruyz*, Año 1622."

Pero siendo asi que la pieza inserta à continuacion, y la de la dicha P^te^ VI (que consta de sueltas) sean una misma, equivoca Barrera en atribuyendola a *Valdivielso*; (cuya Comedia, inserta en el libro citado, de que despues de hecha esta coleccion, he tenido la fortuna de obtenir [sic] un ejemplar), y es obra totalmente distinta de la que aqui se presenta como de Calderon: – y que hasta lograr à descubrir su verdadero Autor, debe pasar por anónima.'

Chorley is correct: Valdivielso's play opens with the line 'Defendido, y verde muro'; and our play does indeed appear in the *Sexta parte* of Saragossa, 1653 (see above, p. 145, copies in Toledo and Vienna). In his description of the Toledo copy of our play, Juliá states that it is also different from Don Juan de Matos Fragoso's *La devoción del ángel de la guarda* (xix, 569–70). The Matos play appeared in his *Primera parte de comedias* (Madrid, 1658), and documents transcribed in Varey and Shergold's *Fuentes para la historia del teatro en España*, iv, London, 1973, mention it as a new play in 1657–8 and suggest that it was performed by Francisco García on 22 February 1658 (see pp. 123, 228). This does not help us to identify the author of our play; by way of compensation, we describe Pennsylvania 623 (Harrach 10):

EL ANGEL DE LA GVARDA. | COMEDIA FAMOSA | DE DOM [sic] PEDRO CALDERON. | Hablan en ella las perſonas ſiguientes. | [Persons in italics – three columns] | IORNADA PRIMERA.

[Begins] *Salen Carlos y Paſqnin.* [sic]

Car. Si es la vida natural
tan caduca fantaſia,

4°. A–D4. No page numbers.

[Running headlines – verso] *El Angel de la Guarda.*
A1v, A3v, A4v, B1v, B3v.
El Angel de la Guarda
A2v, B4v, C3v.
El Angel de al guarda.
B2v.
El Angel de la Cuarda,
C1v.
El Angel de la Guarda,
Remainder, D1v almost illegible.

[Running headlines – recto] *De Don Pedro Calderon.*
All but A4r, C1r.
De Don P edro Calderon.
A4r.
De Don Pedro Calderon
C1r.

[Catchwords] A4v: [cropped] B4v: le [?] C4v: ſi

[Ends] los ſuplais por los deſeos,
ſi ſon prendas que lo valen.
FIN

The text roman is not easily measured from the film, but it is Granjon's *gros cicéro* (our R28) with two-dot js; the italic is our IT9. We are not *absolutely* sure who printed this *suelta*, but we suggest that interested parties should invite Bernardo de Hervada of Madrid to assist them in their enquiries; its types match those used in his edition of Calderón's *Quarta parte* (1674).

Sueltas in the B.L.: 11728.h.14(19), ?Madrid, ?1700; and 11728.a.63, ?Madrid, ?1700. These differ, but one is a page-for-page reprint of the other. Also Biblioteca Apostolica Vaticana, R.G.Lett.est.IV 300, int.6: n.p., n.d., 32pp.

Pepys 1553(22), pp. 701–31 · *Gaselee*, 31

EL MEJOR PADRE DE POBRES. | COMEDIA FAMOSA, | *DE DON PEDRO CALDERON.* | Hablan en ella las perſonas ſiguientes. | [Persons in three columns – italics] | [rule in sixteen sections] | [two hands M12] JORNADA PRIMERA. [two hands M12] [Begins] *Sale San Juan de Dios de ſoldado, con votas, y eſ-|puelas, enſangrentada la cabeza, baxando la | eminencia de vn riſco.*

S.Iu. F Vgitivo corzel, ſañuda fiera,
cuyo indomito ardor, cuya carrera . . .

4°. A–D4. No page numbers. Last page blank.

[Running headlines – verso] *El mejor Padre de Pobres.*
All but A2^v, C3^v, D3^v.
El mejor Padrr de Pobres.
A2^v.
El mejor Padre de pobres.
C3^v, D3^v.

[Running headlines – recto] *De don Pedro Calderon.*

[Catchwords] A4^v: quan- B4^v: *Buelve* C4^v: venir

[Ends] dando fin à la Comedia,
pide vn victor de limoſna.
F I N.

[Final ornament W2]

[Juan Cabezas, *c.* 1678]

Chorley, in a note to B.L. 11728.h.14(14) says: '*El mejor Padre de pobres: y (Medél.) S. Juan de Dios. "de Calderon"*. Es muy cierto no ser esta obra de *Calderon*; con cuyo nombre supuesto va en la P^{te} 15 de *Comedias Escogidas* [Madrid, 1661]: – y corre tambien en impresiones Sueltas. Es una de las piezas que cita Vera Tasis como supuestas: *"en el Juego de Varios"*.

Segun Medél es de Montalbán; y asi la cita Barrera [p. 268a]: – Advertido [¿a?] este le parece esto algun tanto dudoso: – pero no hallando otro dueño, podra pasar "ad interim" por suya.'

In his *Quarta parte* of 1672 Calderón mentioned a play called *San Juan de Dios* as in print and attributed to him, but not by him.

In M. Gómez-Moreno's *Primicias históricas de San Juan de Dios*, Madrid, 1950, there are some reports of plays on this saint's life, pp. 312–14, and on Lope's play *Juan de Dios y Antón Martín*, pp. 328–30.

Professor V. F. Dixon sends us the following note:

'I have seen no play published under this title as Montalbán's, although one was listed as his by both Medel and Huerta. Fajardo, on the other hand, listed *El mejor padre de pobres* as by Calderón, with the alternative title *San Juan de Dios*. He was referring to a play about St John of God entitled *El mejor padre de pobres* and published as Calderón's in *Escogidas 15* and in *sueltas*. [He adds more details already summarised above, and refers to Restori's statement that the *suelta* attributed to Calderón was essentially the same play as José de Arroyo's *El pobre más poderoso San Juan de Dios* (autograph MS preserved in the Biblioteca Palatina, Parma, with licences for 1691; three more MSS in the B.N.M.: 14.999, 16.570 and 17.114. For Restori, see *Zeitschrift für romanische Philologie*, xxii (1898), 278.). Dixon points out that this is an exaggeration, but that Arroyo's play is a *refundición* of the 'Calderón' one, presumably made at the time of the saint's canonization in 1690. He continues:]

[Perhaps this *suelta*] is to be identified instead with a play otherwise now lost, attributed to Antonio Fajardo y Acevedo, *San Juan limosnero, ó el gran padre de pobres* (La Barrera, p. 149a). It must not be confused, though, with either Rodrigo Pacheco's *El mejor padre de pobres* [the second play of a trilogy on St Francis of Assisi – in B.N.M., MS/14.824, Paz y Melia 2340] or Lope's *Juan de Dios y Antón Martín*.

[The *suelta*] may have been the play attributed to Montalbán; but if so, there is little reason to think that the attribution was correct. Nothing in its style, construction or characterization suggests that Montalbán was the author.'

Professor Dixon adds – with regard to the manuscript in B.N.M. described in Paz y Melia 2341, which has the incipit and ending of our *suelta* – 'This [manuscript], not attributed to any author, . . . is merely a faithful eighteenth-century copy of the *Escogidas* text.' [B.N.M., MS/19.675]

Signora Profeti lists the following *sueltas* (pp. 466–8):

B.L., 11728.b.39, another copy of Pepys 1553(22), although the General Catalogue's guess-date is ?1720.

B.L., 11728.h.14(14); B.N.M., U/10340; Österreichische Nationalbibliothek, Vienna, 442.280–B; Biblioteca Palatina, Parma, CC*IV 28033, vol. xxvii: n.p., n.d., 20 unnumbered leaves signed A–E4. A possible fifth copy in the University Library, Barcelona, cannot now be traced.

B.N.M., T/4443 and T/i/120[16]; Instituto del Teatro, Barcelona, 39796; Universitätsbibliothek, Freiburg, E–1032–n–VII; Toronto 432: like the previous *suelta*, but with serial number 191. We also know of a *suelta* in the Uppsala University Library (Br. Litt. Hisp., n.p., n.d.), but we have no further details.

Pepys 1553(23), pp. 733–64 · *Gaselee*, 179

LA OBEDIENCIA LAVREADA. | COMEDIA FAMOSA, | DE LOPE DE VEGA CARPIO. | Hablan en ella las perſonas ſiguientes. | [Persons in italics – three columns] | [line of ornaments M1]

[Begins] JORNADA PRIMERA. | *Suena dentro ruydo de pendencia, como* | *caſa de juego.*

Fil. BAſta que lo diga yo.
Ale. Miẽte, ſi lo dize. *Fi.* Muera . . .

4°. [A–D4?] Signatures ravaged by binder's knife. No page numbers.

[Running headlines – verso] La Obediencia Lavreada.
A1v, B1v, B2v, B3v, C3v.

La Obediencia lavreada.
A2^{v}.
La obediencia Lavreada.
A3^{v}.
La Obediencia Lavbreada.
C4^{v}.
Y primer Carlos de Vngria.
A4^{v}, B4^{v}, C1^{v}, C2^{v},
D1^{v}, D2^{v}, D3^{v}, D4^{v}.

[Running headlines – recto] Y primer Carlos de Vngria.
A2^{r}, B1^{r}, B3^{r}, C3^{r}.
Y primer Carlos de Vngria
A3^{r}.
Y primer Carlos de Vngri.
A4^{r}, B2^{r}, C4^{r}.
La obediencia Lavreada.
B4^{r}, D1^{r}, D2^{r}.
La Obediencia Lavreada.
C1^{r}, C2^{r}.
La obedencia Lavreada.
D3^{r}, D4^{r}.

[Catchwords unreadable, except on C4^{v}] porque

[Ends] la Obediencia Laureada,
y primer Carlos de Vngria.
F I N.

[Tomé de Dios Miranda, *c.* 1678]

Printed in Lope's *Parte VI* of 1615 (approved 1614). According to Morley and Bruerton, an 'authentic undated play', possible dates range between 1597 and 1606, but probably 1604–06 (p. 226). La Barrera lists it on p. 441a with the full title *La obediencia laureada, y primer Carlos de Hungría.*

Paz y Melia records a manuscript in the B.N.M.: MS/16.871. 'Letra del siglo xvii.' (item 2653)

Four copies of a *suelta* of Madrid, Theresa de Guzmán, n.d.: B.L. 11728.f.72 and 11728.h.6(19), guess-date ?1730; Bibliothèque Nationale, Paris, 8° Yg.1308(105); Wayne State 399.

Cf. Ada M. Coe, *Catálogo bibliográfico y crítico de las comedias anunciadas en los periódicos de Madrid desde 1661 hasta 1819*, Baltimore, Maryland, etc., 1935, p. 169: '*La obediencia laureada, y primer Carlos de Ungria*, por Lope de Vega, Lonja de Comedias de la Puerta del Sol, 13 dic. 1735 (Gaceta).' Another, 36 pp., n.p., n.d., Whitney, p. 394a.

La obediencia laureada was reprinted in the fourth volume of Lope de Vega's *Comedias*, edited by Juan Eugenio Hartzenbusch (*Biblioteca de Autores Españoles*, lii) and in the thirteenth volume of the second series published by the Real Academia Española.

Pepys 1553(24), pp. 765–91 · *Gaselee*, 153

NO AY DICHA, NI DESDICHA HASTA LA MVERTE. | COMEDIA | FAMOSA, | *DE DON FRANCISCO DE ROXAS.* | Hablan en ella las perſonas ſiguientes. | [Persons in italics – three columns] | [rule in fifteen sections] | [two hands M12] JORNADA PRIMERA. [two hands M12]

[Begins] *Tocan arma, y ſalen con rodelas, y eſpa-|das deſnudas, cada vno por ſu puerta,* | *Don Diego Porzelos, D Vela y* | *Mangana, y Carraſco,* | *gracioſos.*

Vel. Pienſo que al arma han tocado.

Porz. Las hueſtes de D. Garcia . . .

4°. A–C4 D2. No page numbers. Last page blank.

[Running headlines – verso] *De Don Franciſco de Roxas.*

[Running headlines – recto] *No ay dicha, ni deſdicha haſta la muerte.*

[Catchwords] A4v: *Viol.* Ya, B4v: como C4v: no

[Ends] y aſſi ſe vé, que en el mundo
no ay dicha, ni deſdicha haſta la muerte.

F I N.

[Final ornament W4]

[Juan Cabezas, *c.* 1678]

According to J. Simón Díaz, *Bibliografía*, iv, no. 245, this play was printed in *Comedias escogidas XLV* of 1679, attributed to 'un Ingenio desta Corte'. It was attributed to Mira de Amescua by Mesonero Romanos in *Biblioteca de Autores Españoles*, xlv, 39. Salvá (i, 629b) hesitated between Rojas Zorrilla and Mira de Amescua. La Barrera quoted an Osuna manuscript attributed to Mira – and this is now Paz y Melia 2555: 'Comedia del Dr. Mira de Amescua. Autógrafa y firmada en Madrid a 20 de julio de 1628. Para Andrés de la Vega. Licencias en Madrid, de 17 [sic, for 12, see below] de abril de 1629, y Granada 8 de noviembre de 1636. B.N.M. Res. 76'. MacCurdy describes it as 'apócrifa: es de Mira de Amescua' (*op. cit.* in notes to 1553[12], p. 147). Any lingering doubts seem to be dispelled by Vern G. Williamsen in his edition published by the University of Missouri Press (Columbia, 1970). Attributing the play firmly to Mira, he corrects Paz y Melia's misreading of the date of the first *licencia*, and points out that the 'autograph' manuscript is only partly in Mira's hand. He refers to another B.N.M. manuscript, MS/14.920, with licences of April 1685, and to a *refundición* in the Biblioteca Municipal, Madrid, made for performances in 1781 and 1787. He lists the following *sueltas*: B.L. [T.1740(9), ?Madrid, ?1650], with another copy in the National Library at Vienna. This is apparently different from an imprintless *suelta* in the Bibliothèque Nationale, Paris [Yg.347(1)]. Finally there is one attributed to Mira of Madrid, Antonio Sanz, 1748, at N. Carolina [1302]. We can add further copies of the last in the Bibliothèque Nationale (Yg.488), at Wayne State (387), and in the collection of Mr Bruno Scarfe. Under Rojas, the Bibliothèque Nationale catalogues another imprintless *suelta*: Yg.345(3), 4°, 16 leaves.

Mr Scarfe has another *suelta*, possibly of the seventeenth century, and sends us this description:

[Tear] MEDIA FAMOSA | [Tear] O AY DICHA, NI DESDICHA, | haſta la muerte. | DE DON FRANCISCO DE ROXAS. | Hablan en ella las perſonas ſiguientes. | [Persons in italics – three columns] | IORNADA PRIMERA.

[Begins] *Tocan al arma, y ſalen con rodelas, y eſ-|padas deſnudas cada vno por ſu puerta,* | *D. Diego Porcelos D. Vela, y Monga-|na, y Carraſco gracioſos.*

Vel. Pienſo que al arma hã tocado.

Por. Las hueſtes de don Garcia . . .

4°. A–D4. No page numbers.

[Running headlines – verso] *No ay dicha, ni deſdicha, haſta la muerte.* All but A4v, C1v.

De Don Francèſco de Roxas. A4v.

No ay dicha, ni deſdicha haſta la muerte. C1v.

[Running headlines – recto] *De Don Franciſco de Roxas.* All.

[Catchwords] A4v: *Rey.* B4v: eſte C4v: ha-

[Ends] no ay dicha, ni deſdicha,
haſta la muerte.
FIN.

Pepys 1553(25), pp. 793–824 · *Gaselee*, 155

LOS TRABAJOS DE TOBIAS. | La nueua. | COMEDIA FAMOSA | DE DON FRANCISCO DE ROXAS. | Hablan en ella las perſonas ſiguientes. | [Persons in italics – three columns] | IORNADA PRIMERA.

[Begins] *Sale Gabeleo.* [sic]

Gab. Maldiga el cielo tu campo,
ingrato pueblo ſin Dios, . . .

4°. A–D4. No page numbers.

[Running headlines – verso] *Los trabajos de Tobias.* All but A2v, B1v.

Los trabajos de Tobias A2v, B1v.

[Running headlines – recto] *De Don Franciſco de Roxas.* All but A2^r, B1^r, B2^r, B3^r, B4^r.
De Don Franciſco de Rojas. A2^r, B1^r, B2^r, B3^r, B4^r.

[Catchwords] A4^v: ay B4^v: que C4^v: Aza-

[Ends] licencia para otra pide,
y para eſta pide vn vitor.
F I N.

[Tomé de Dios Miranda, *c.* 1675]

There appear to be two versions of this play, both attributed to Rojas Zorrilla: this one, called 'La nueua', and another without that addition. The former – that of our *suelta* – is that printed in the *Parte treinta y tres de doze comedias famosas de varios autores*, Valencia, 1642 (Simón Díaz, *Bibliografía*, iv, no. 264), in the *Parte segunda* of Rojas (Madrid, 1645 and 1680), and in the *Doze comedias nueuas de diferentes autores las mejores que hasta aora han salido . . . Parte XXXXXVII* of 'Valencia, 1646' (referred to above, pp. 68 and 157). According to Restori's description of the *suelta*, it has sixteen leaves, all of them signed. There is also a manuscript of this version of the play, copied in Madrid by Matías de Morales on 24 April 1712 (B.N.M., MS/16.674, Paz y Melia 3575). Two B.L. *sueltas*: C.108.bbb. 20(13), n.p., n.d., guess-date ?1700; and 1342.f.1(27), guess-date ?Madrid, ?1755, second copy at 11728.h.19(19).

The (presumably) older version begins with the line: 'Viua el gran Senaquerib'. There are the following *sueltas* of it:
Madrid, Antonio Sanz, 1755: Toronto 652, Bainton 788.
Barcelona, Viuda Piferrer, n.d.: Bainton 787 (U.L.C. guess-date ?1780), Moll 1127, N. Carolina 1766, Pennsylvania 2923.

R. R. MacCurdy does not distinguish between these two plays in his works on Rojas Zorrilla.

Readers of Pepys's *Diary* may recall the fact that on the Lord's Day 1660 he attended divine service, where 'A stranger preached a poor sermon, and so I read over the whole book of the story of Tobit'. (Wheatley's edition, i [1893], 45; R. Latham and W. Matthews's edition, i [1970], 42.)

Pepys 1553(26), pp. 825–56 · *Gaselee*, 133

SANTA MARIA EGIPCIACA, | Y GITANA DE MENFIS. | COMEDIA FAMOSA. | DEL DOCTOR IVAN PEREZ DE MONTALVAN. | Hablan en ella las perſonas ſiguientes. | [Persons in italics – three columns] | [line of ornaments M5, M7, M8]

[Begins] IORNADA PRIMERA. | *Salen Maria, y Teodora de Gitanas, y Iu|lio, Celio, y Ricardo de galanes, y* | *tocan caxas deſtem-|pladas*

Iul. El peſame, Maria bella,
  os damos los tres *Mar.* De que? . . .

4º. A–D4. No page numbers.

[Running headlines – verso] La Gitana de Menfis. All but A4ᵛ, B2ᵛ, C4ᵛ, D3ᵛ.
La Gitrana de Menfis. A4ᵛ, B2ᵛ, C4ᵛ, D3ᵛ.

[Running headlines – recto] Del Doctor Iuan Perez de Montalvan. All but A2ʳ, B2ʳ, C4ʳ, D4ʳ.
Del Doctor Iuan perez de Montalvan. A2ʳ, B2ʳ, C4ʳ, D4ʳ.

[Catchwords] A4ᵛ: el B4ᵛ: ſino C4ᵛ: Que

[Ends] de la Gitana de Menfis,
  Santa Maria Egipciac. [sic]
  F I N.

[Tomé de Dios Miranda, *c.* 1675]

Apart from a manuscript in the Biblioteca Municipal, Madrid, which not even Signora Profeti was able to examine, the play exists only in *sueltas*, of which there are a great many (listed by her on pp. 259–64). There is a record of a performance at court by Pedro de Ortegón on 6 November 1636 (Shergold and Varey, 'Some palace performances of seventeenth-century plays', p. 237). The author's name is not mentioned.

Professor Dixon tells us that there are a few resemblances to scenes or incidents in the authentic plays of Montalbán, but he hesitates to attribute the play to him. He also sends some curious details about the suppression of the play by the Inquisition in 1795–6 and the issue of a purged edition called *Pecadora y penitente Santa Maria Egipciaca.* (The manuscript listed by Signora Profeti [p. 264] with the title *La pecadora penitente* and a *censura* of 20 February 1808 seems to be of this version. It is now in the Biblioteca Municipal, Madrid.)

Signora Profeti lists the following *sueltas* apart from the Pepys one:

Instituto del Teatro, Barcelona: n.p., n.d., A–D^4; no. 60792.

British Library, 1072.h.15(4): n.p., n.d., A–D^4 E^2; another copy in the London Library, P.912(2).

Österreichische Nationalbibliothek, Vienna: n.p., n.d., A–D^4 E^2; two copies, +38.V.4(5) and +38.V.4(9).

Biblioteca Palatina, Parma: n.p., n.d., A–D^4 E^2; CC*II.28056, vol. iv.

Instituto del Teatro, Barcelona: n.p., n.d., A–D^4; no. 58861.

Biblioteca Nazionale Marciana, Venice: n.p., n.d., A–C^4 D^2; 110.C.28.3.

Biblioteca de la Universidad, Santiago de Compostela: n.p., n.d., A^4–E^2 [sic; A–D^4 E^2?]

Instituto del Teatro, Barcelona: n.p., n.d., A–D^4 E^1; no. 60171.

Signora Profeti did not see the Santiago *suelta*, or two imprintless *sueltas* in Boston Public Library (D.171.3.2) and the Hispanic Society of America. To this group we can add Pennsylvania 712, n.p., n.d. (Harrach 17). Those with an imprint:

Toronto 292: Seville, widow of Francisco de Leefdael, n.d. (recorded as Aguilar Piñal 1621). A–D^4.

Bibliothèque Nationale, Paris: Seville, M. N. Vázquez, n.d., A–C^4 D^2; 8° Yg.1401(17).

B.N.M., T/15013(13): Valladolid, A. del Riego, n.d., A–D4; other copies in the Biblioteca Municipal, Madrid, Instituto del Teatro, Barcelona (no. 33918) and the London Library (P. 1121). We can add a fifth in the Archivo Histórico Nacional, Madrid, and the information that these are not all of one edition.

Instituto del Teatro, Barcelona: Salamanca, Imprenta de la Santa Cruz, n.d., [A–D4] (imperfect); no. 61744. We know of another imperfect copy, B.N.M., T–i/151.

B.N.M., T/5828: Madrid, A. Sanz, 1738, A–D4; another copy, Biblioteca Palatina, Parma, CC*II. 28056, vol. i.

Real Academia Española: Madrid, A. Sanz, 1748, A–D4 (i.e. Moll 479); another copy, Biblioteca de la Universidad, Valencia, A–110/69, imperfect.

B.N.M., U/1077: Madrid, A. Sanz, 1756, A–D4; other copies in Instituto del Teatro, Barcelona (nos. 39655 and 57905), Biblioteca de la Universidad, Valencia, A–104/102, Bibliothèque Nationale, Paris, Yg.415, B.L., 1342.e.12(29) and 11728.h.13(7), Boston Public Library, G.3354.3, London Library, P.984. We can add a tenth, Pennsylvania 1756.

Bibliothèque Nationale, Paris: Salamanca, F. de Toxar, 1792, A–D4: 8° Yg. Pièce 609; another copy, Universitätsbibliothek, Freiburg, E–1032–n–XXI.

Pepys 1553(27), pp. 857–903 · *Gaselee*, 139

[Title page] VEJAMEN | CON QVE SE AFECTÓ | EL REGOZIJO DEL CVMPLIMIENTO | DE AñOS DE NVESTRO REY, Y SEñOR | D. CARLOS II. | EN EL GRADO QVE DE DOCT. | EN SAGRADA THEOLOGIA RECIBIO | EL REVERENDISSIMO PADRE | DIEGO DE CASTEL-BLANCO, | VISITADOR GENERAL DE SV RELIGION, DE LOS PA-|dres Clerigos Menores, y predicador de ſu Mageſtad en el Colegio Mayor | de Santa Maria de Iesvs, Vniverſidad de Sevilla. |

VIERNES DIA VEINTE Y SIETE DE DIZIEMBRE | DEL AñO DE 1675. | SIENDO SEñOR RECTOR IVEZ CANCILLER | DE DICHO COLEGIO, Y VNIUERSIDAD | EL SEÑOR D. D. BARTOLOME | DE LA SERNA, | CATEDRATICO DE UISPERAS DE CANONES. | *COMPVESTO, Y DADO* | POR EL DOCT. D. FRANCISCO | DE PRADA, | CATREDATICO [sic] DE VISPERAS DE MEDICINA. | *DEDICALE SV AVTOR.* | AL EX^MO^. SEñOR DON PEDRO ANDRES DE GVZMAN, | Comendador del Orden de Santiago, de la Eſpada de Caſtilla, Marques de | la Algava, Conde de Teba, y Ardales, Cauallerizo primero de ſu Ma-|geſtad, que Dios guarde.

4°. A–F4. [1–3] 4–32 35 34–47 [48] = 48 pages. Verso of title-page and last page blank.

[A2^r^] [Copper-plate depiction of four symbolic figures supporting three spheres and a crown, headed: GEROGLIFICO D[E] LA EDAD DE CARLOS. II. The three spheres represent the (almost complete) three lustra of the age of Charles II, who was born in 1661. Inscribed on a surrounding circle are the names of the virtues depicted or symbolised: LEALTAD ESPAÑOLA. LA FELICIDAD. ARMAS Y LETRAS. EL TIENPO. EL DERECHO NATVRAL. The engraving is signed: Mat[ias de] Artiaga f[ecit] A[nn]o [16]75. Artiaga (or Arteaga) worked from at least 1663 to 1703 in Seville. Some of his best work can be seen in Torre Farfán's *Fiestas* of Seville, 1671 (referred to above, p. 20). Under the engraving is a poem in *octavas reales* which explains the device]

Firme, de la lealtad, piadoſo el zelo
En obſequio de Carlos, ya imagina . . .

[Ends on A3^v^. On A4^r^ and A4^v^ are two acrostic sonnets in honour of Charles II; the first letter in each line is printed horizontally to read: EDADES, TRIVNFOS A CARLOS SEGVNDO.]

[B1^r^] A EL EXCELENTISSIMO SEÑOR | DON

PEDRO ANDRES | DE GUZMAN, | Comendador . . .

[Begins] N[W6]*o á todo linage de cariño entibiò la auſencia, como ni* . . .

[Ends] *El Doctor D. Franciſco de Prada.*

[B2^r] [line of ornaments M14] | PASSEO DE LA VNIVERSIDAD.

[Begins] E[W7]n ocaſion de la celebridad publica por el cumpli-| . . .

[Ends on B4^v. Final ornament W2]

[C1^r] [line of ornaments M13] | INTRODVCCION. | *Poneſe el Bejante, y ſaca vn guiſopo mojado en agua maldita* | *y echando aſperges dize.*

A[W5]Spergimini cum iſto guiſopandorio. El ſeñor Rec-| . . .

[Ends on F4^r, p. 47]

[Juan Cabezas, ?1676]

Recorded by Simón Díaz, *Impresos del siglo XVII*, 2374; he quotes two copies in B.N.M.

Pepys 1553(28), pp. 905–44 · *Gaselee*, 95

[Title page] VEJAMEN | CON QVE SE CELEBRO EL GRADO | QUE DE DOCTOR EN SAGRADA THEOLOGIA | RECIBIO EL M. R. P. PRESENTADO | Fr. FRANCISCO | LVIS GARCIA, | RELIGIOSO DEL SAGRADO ORDEN DE NVESTRA | Señora del Carmen, Lector de Prima del Inſigne | Colegio de S. Alberto. | EN EL COLEGIO MAYOR DE SANTA MARIA DE JESVS | CELEBRE VNIVERSIDAD DE SEVILLA*;* | MIERCOLES DIA VEINTE Y NUEVE DE ABRIL | del Año de 1682. | SIENDO SEÑOR RECTOR JVEZ CANCILLER DE DICHO | COLEGIO, Y VNIVERSIDA*D* | EL SEÑOR DON JVAN BEXINES | Y VEGA, | DOCTOR EN

SAGRADA THEOLOGIA. | *COMPVESTO, Y DADO* | POR D. CHRISTOVAL FRANCISCO | DE LVQUE, | DOCTOR EN LA FACVLTAD DE MEDICINA. | DEDICALE SV AVTOR AL SEñOR D. JVAN BALTASAR FEDERIGUI | Cavallero del Orden de Santiago, Conde de Villanueva, y General de la Armada | de Flota que va â Nueva-Eſpaña. | [line of ornaments M15] | IMPRESSO EN SEVILLA POR JVAN FRANCICO [sic] DE BLAS, | Impreſſor mayor de dicha Ciudad. | Acoſta de PEDRO DE SANTIAGO, Mercader de Libros, vende en ſu caſa, en la Papele-|ria, en frente de la Carcel de los ſeñores.

4°. A–E4. Foliated: [i–iv] 1–7 [blank] 9–16 = iv+16 fols. Verso of title-page blank.

[A2^r] + | AL SEÑOR | D. JUAN BALTASAR FEDERIGUI, | Cavallero . . .

[Begins] D[W9]*iſculpe vn atrevimiento, no de* | . . .

[Ends] *El Doct. D. Chriſtoval Franciſco* | *de Luque.*

[A3^r] PASSEO DE LA VNIVERSIDAD. | Para la celebridad deſte feſtejo ſe adornô el patio de | . . .

[B1^r] Fol. I. | [oblong pattern of ornaments M16 containing the monogram IHS] | INTRODVCCION. | E[W10]a Señores, y Señoras mias, ya cumpliendo . . .

[Final ornament W8 on E4^v, fol. 16^v]

Recorded by Santiago Montoto, *Impresos sevillanos*, no. 209, though no copy is cited.

INDEXES

We hoped, when we prepared this monograph, that it would be of interest to historians of typography and of Spanish Golden-Age drama. Accordingly, we have provided a separate index to cater for each of these interests: an index of persons involved in the book trade, and an index of authors and works. The professions (printer, bookseller. etc.) added to the names in the book trade list are not intended to be complete definitions: they relate only to the activities dealt with in this text. Thus Robert Granjon is described simply as a punchcutter. Similarly, the listing of particular designs of type under the name of a foundry means only that these designs were at some time available from that foundry; it does not necessarily mean that they originated there or that they were available nowhere else. In the author index, we have followed usual practice in listing an author's complete works, partial collections, authentic single works and supposititious single works, in that order. Collected volumes of plays in which one author's name figures on the title-page will be found under that author. Collected volumes with no such name on the title-page are to be found under *partes de comedias*, and anonymous works under their titles.

INDEX OF PERSONS INVOLVED IN THE BOOK TRADE

INDEX OF AUTHORS AND WORKS CITED IN THE TEXT